The Last Hunter

Harold Weaver, 1941

The Last Hunter

AN AMERICAN FAMILY ALBUM

Will Weaver

BOREALIS
BOOKS

Borealis Books is an imprint of the Minnesota Historical Society Press.

www.borealisbooks.org

The Minnesota Historical Society Press is a member of the Association of American University Presses.

Manufactured in the United States of America

10 9 8 7 6 5 4 3 2 1

♾ The paper used in this publication meets the minimum requirements of the American National Standard for Information Sciences—Permanence for Printed Library Materials, ANSI Z39.48-1984.

International Standard Book Number
ISBN: 978-0-87351-776-8 (cloth)
ISBN: 978-0-87351-811-6 (e-book)

Library of Congress Cataloging-in-Publication Data

Weaver, Will.
The last hunter : an American family album / Will Weaver.
p.   cm.
ISBN 978-0-87351-776-8 (cloth : alk. paper) —
ISBN 978-0-87351-811-6 (e-book)
1. Deer hunting—Minnesota. 2. Fowling—Minnesota. 3. Hunters—Minnesota—Social life and customs. 4. Weaver family.   I. Title.
SK301.W347   2010
799.292—dc22
[B]
2010023349

To my family.
Everywhere.

The Last Hunter

Chapter One

My mother, Arlys, was born in 1920. Her parents, Oscar and Sarah Swenson, came from North Dakota and landed northeast of Detroit Lakes, Minnesota, on one of the last patches of the Great Plains. Locally the area is called the Ponsford Prairie; geographically it has the empty feel of North Dakota. The farm had a narrow white house, white barn, wooden granary, chicken coop, machine shed, and well house; a windbreak to the west; a thin scattering of imported trees, including a row of lilacs in the yard. North Dakotans tend to cut down trees in order to name streets after them, but on my grandfather's farm there were no trees to fuss about: unbroken fields stretched in all directions as flat and wide as God's dinner plate. However, four miles to the south were the Smoky Hills, their rounded crowns blurred by hardwood and aspen, and just east of the farm the beginning of pine and lake country, with forests that stretched across northern Minnesota and Wisconsin and into Michigan. If my mother paused on the front steps of the farmhouse and looked about, a dark tree line would have circumscribed most of her little prairie.

In the fall, when Canada geese came through and when partridge season opened, she heard the far-off thudding report of shotguns, and in November the heavier *poom-poom!* of deer rifles in the hills. However, hunting seasons were not important to her or her two brothers. On the Swenson side of my family, there were no guns.

Oscar Swenson, my grandfather, was born in the south of Norway in 1894 and emigrated with his family in 1898. One of his earliest memories was of delivering water to "rich men" on the deck of the passenger ship. I imagine him as a Dickensian boy, hat in hand, wearing a rough wool shirt as he carries a water pail toward a man in a deck chair. The man is wrapped in a blanket against the salt chill; perhaps he wears muttonchops below a tall hat and is having a bowl of tobacco. Maybe he is reading. There's a good chance he is annoyed at the little boy offering a wooden ladle full of water, or perhaps he is seasick, as the ship leans through heavy seas and the seagulls bark overhead and, grateful, he fishes out a coin for my grandfather. This is the ending I prefer, but the encounter itself is the thing—a transaction weighted with issues of wealth, class, and privilege.

In 1989, when I was thirty-nine, I heard the *Hjemkomst* call. I had a sabbatical from teaching, and my children were eleven and eight years old, ages that felt like a momentary respite from close parenting. Carrying with me information provided by my mother, who is the history keeper in our family, I flew from Minneapolis to Oslo. From there I continued by train to Kristiansand in the south of Norway; then by bus twenty kilometers northward along the narrowing Otra

River, which flows to the sea; and finally east a jog to the village of Vennesla.

The morning after my arrival, and following a fine Norwegian breakfast of smoked salmon, scrambled eggs, lingonberry jam on rye bread, and dark coffee, I explained my quest to the innkeeper. Arny was a thinning-haired blondish fellow—like most Scandinavians, older than he looked—and when I showed him a faded, black-and-white photo of my great-grandfather Carl Swenson's house, his pale blue eyes lit up. In Norway (and in Ireland, my wife says), there is no greater way to create a stir and make friends than to arrive from America in search of family. Facebook has nothing on an original photo of the "home place."

Arny made some calls, and distant relatives showed up within the half hour and carted me off for a couple of whirlwind days of eating: smørbrød (open sandwiches), gravlaks (raw, cured salmon with dill), sliced and dressed cucumbers, sild (pickled herring), Jarlsberg cheese, and all manner of sweets—krumkake, kringles, and rosettes. No lutefisk, thank God. After the initial hum and buzz, and as I got to know my long-lost relatives and hear their stories, I came to the conclusion that I knew in my bones: my great-grandfather had left Norway because of the rich men. They who controlled the rights to salmon fishing in the rivers and streams. They who owned the precious five percent of Norway's arable land. They who hunted and, of course, owned guns.

Anton Chekhov, the Russian writer, was also a physician. But he came from peasant stock on one side of his family and wrote of "squeezing the slave from himself drop by drop"—with the implication that he never quite succeeded. My grandfather became a landowner and a modestly successful farmer in the American Midwest, but he never owned a gun. Guns were for other kinds of men.

His family arrived at Ellis Island in 1898. My great-grandfather shepherded them by train east through Chicago and Wisconsin, bypassing the rich farmland of Iowa and southern Minnesota as he made his way to northeastern North Dakota, where there were sufficient rocks, trees, and Norwegians. My great-grandfather's homestead farm was four hundred and some acres, including most of a small lake, on the eastern edge of the aptly named Turtle Mountains. While nothing like the steep cliffs and fjords of Norway, the rounded, pine-covered hills with their feet mudded into small lakes and sloughs must have been of some comfort to him.

Emigration has a different affect upon different generations, but in terms of mental health it has to be toughest on the first. Friends and family members have been left behind. There is a new language, new manners to learn, plaguing second thoughts about the wisdom of the decision to leave home, discouraging New World days filled with *sorg* and *lengsel*—with sadness and longing.

Among midwestern Scandinavians, the second generation, in its drive to assimilate, forgot the old country in a calculated, even determined manner. Children of immigrants wanted nothing much to do with the old ways. They were embarrassed by their old-fashioned parents, their ears were stopped against the old language, they wanted to dress like—wanted to be—American children. As adults, they kept the battered steamer trunk in the attic and did not make rosettes or lefse or celebrate Norwegian Independence Day. This pattern seems different with modern immigrants—the Hmong in Minnesota, for example, who keep their cultural traditions brightly at hand no matter what the generation—but the

Norwegians in my family turned their faces resolutely forward until they, suddenly, were middle-aged. Then they made a late effort to remember. Some took lessons in Norwegian for their trip back "home"; the steamer trunk was brought down from the attic, painted on the outside and lined inside with flower-patterned, adhesive-backed paper, and displayed in the living room (trunks are great places to store quilts). At least one person in the family took a rosemaling class. Rosettes returned to the Christmas dinner table. My sister Judy took my mother, then in her eighties, to Norway; it was their first visit to the Old Country, and for my mother it filled in important pieces of family history. "Better late than never," she remarked of the trip.

The third and fourth generations (me, depending upon how one counts) make well-meaning attempts to remember, but the going gets tougher. Against the tide of telephones, television, and consumer culture—the homogenization of America, as Eric Sevareid described in his essay "Velva, North Dakota"—it is increasingly difficult to hold on to an inherited cultural past. For my children, Norway is a faded family mirror of story fragments, keepsakes, and tattered photos of narrow houses and workhorses and people without names. As each generation passes, the hard edges of the emigrant experience, like stones washed by waves, are buffed smoother and more featureless. The drafty farmhouse, the kerosene lamps, the low-ceilinged barn, the winter "slop jar" in the bedroom—all of it recedes behind modern times, which is midwestern-speak for indoor plumbing. A toilet inside the house came only after the arrival of power and light, but unless you have sat upon the cold, wooden seat of a sagging, outdoor biffy and smelled the dank pit below, it is not fully possible to imagine life without running water, or electricity for that matter. The harshness of early farm life softens under the layering on of time and becomes sentimentalized—call it the Terry Redlin Effect—but I remember well the Swenson homestead farm in northeastern North Dakota.

It was a lonely place in hill country, well out of sight from the gravel road. A few small outbuildings, some built of logs. A pinched, sharp-roofed farmhouse, its white paint long gone gray. A kitchen window, its thin curtain held an inch to the side by someone behind it peering out. If he was in the yard when we arrived, Great-uncle Emil scuttled into a shed or the house as if to hide or secure something. Though they had been notified (one might say warned) that we were coming, no one in the house came out to greet us. After my father had shut off the pickup's engine, we always lingered in the yard by the truck so that the old Swensons could get used to the fact that the Minnesota relatives had arrived.

To the west, just visible through the trees was Jarvis Lake, small and shallow and lined with wild rice beds. It was a perfect place to hunt ducks and geese, but my father never brought along a shotgun—which was a puzzlement to me. "They don't really hunt up here," my father explained once as he looked around the tumbledown yard. "They're kind of different."

Eventually, one or the other of the two unmarried sisters appeared in silhouette behind the screen door and peered out—our signal to approach the house.

My grandfather had five sisters and three brothers. Leonard died as an infant and was buried "just east of the driveway, near the old, three-stick gate, in a small pine coffin made by a neighbor," my mother says. Another brother, Arnold, caught the measles and a chill besides and was never "right" afterward; he was "willful" and "stubborn" and "hard to handle"; eventually he went to an asylum in Jamestown. Mildred went off to teach but never married and eventually returned to the farm, where Emil and Magna and Selma, all of whom also never married, lived out their lives. Selma ventured out briefly in service to a doctor and his family in a nearby town but was "taken advantage of" in a scandal that is still not talked about in my mother's family. Afterward, she came home to stay. Only two sisters, Ida and Hannah, married and left the farm for good, though they only went to Cando, ten miles away, and Fargo, about a two-hour drive. In real ways, then, few of my grandfather's immediate family went very far in life. In 1925, my great-grandfather, Carl Swenson, beaten down by the emigrant experience and exhausted by his large family, waded into the lake and drowned himself.

As a kid, I visited the old homestead out of duty on enforced family trips, but later, as an adult, I went out of curiosity. A need to know more about the Old People, as we called them. My grandfather had worked out on nearby North Dakota grain farms and eventually broke away to Minnesota—his own emigration—where he married and started a farm. From there, a couple of times yearly he made the long trip back home, hauling a pickup load of oats for Emil's workhorse; canned goods, jellies, and produce; or "perfectly good clothes" (mended by my mother) and perhaps new dresses for each of "the girls"—though there was always a question as to whether Magna and Selma would wear anything new. As my mother describes it, "they were slaves to Emil, who ruled the roost." I remember him, my great-uncle, as a lean, bent-over, squinty-eyed man who wore his boots until they had to be wrapped tightly around and around and around with baling twine and who, when he cut down a tree, felt compelled to remove the stump from the ground before he felled another. These tendencies did not accelerate the manifest destiny of the homestead farm.

My mother's family always thought of Emil, Magna, and Selma as charity cases, if stubborn ones. One October in the early 1970s, my parents purchased and delivered to the homestead farm a gas-powered refrigerator. They arranged for the local gas company in Rolla to deliver and hook up a propane tank. After my father made sure that everything worked correctly, my parents returned from North Dakota greatly pleased at this giant leap forward—until two days later, when the fellow from the gas company in Rolla called.

"I went out to the Swenson farm and took back the tank," he said.

"But it's all paid for," my mother said.

"I know," he said, "but they asked me to take it away."

"But why?" my mother asked.

"Said they were afraid of the gas," the man replied. "Said they couldn't sleep at night."

I remember, at our Minnesota Thanksgiving dinner that year, how the gas tank repo had caused a good deal of head shaking and muttering and eventual laughter. My grandfather, when bemused, had a habit of tilting his face to the side and drawing a big thumb across his leading temple as if the gesture helped him think: what, after all, could a person do about the Old People? The joke, finally, was on my grandparents and parents. When the last of the three recluses died and the house was inventoried, among Emil's things was a steamer trunk packed with thousands of dollars in cash.

In the end my grandfather, the most soft-spoken man I've ever known, was the most outgoing member of his family. As an eighth grader, his last year in school, he walked fifty miles south to Cando and waited on Main Street with other grown men to be hired on by the wheat farmers from farther south on the North Dakota prairie. He sent money home every week from the Henry Miller farm where he bunked with other "boys" (men, really) and kept back only a dollar for himself. He pitched wheat bundles onto wagons, then graduated to driving a horse team and wagon that ran the bundles to the big steam-driven threshing machine. At some point during those days he acquired a fundamental, Quaker-like prairie religion, and when he volunteered for World War I, he made it clear that he would not carry a rifle.

There is a photo, taken in 1917 just before they mustered, of my grandfather and seven other young men in their World War I uniforms. All eight are conscientious objectors. Four stand. Four sit below. Their uniforms are tidy and buttoned at the throat. The men face the camera but not squarely or stiffly. They are capless. There is no peacock in their posture, no forced bravado in their expressions. As Wilfred Owen wrote in the most famous poem of World War I, *"Dulce et Decorum Est,"* they are not "ardent" with "high zest" for "some desperate glory." They understand that while it might be fitting and right to die for one's country, it is nothing to smile about. But neither are they afraid. The eight seem remarkably at peace with whatever is to come their way.

It could not have been easy for COs in World War I. My grandfather's job for two years was scullery work in a big hospital in Chicago. It was the time of the great Spanish flu epidemic of 1918, and he remembered "boys stacked like cordwood in the snow behind the hospital." He also got the flu but survived, my mother says, by staying within the high heat of the kitchens and taking their humidity into his lungs. He returned home in 1919 and went back to the wheatfields and the Miller farm, where he met my grandmother.

Sometimes a marriage is a fundamentally bad match, like two colors mixing darkly or two mechanical parts that grind against each other and, over time, wear the other down. But my whole family to come was brightened—its blood quickened—by Sarah Ella Bowen, always known as Ella. My grandmother was born three years before my grandfather, in 1891, in a covered wagon coming up from Nebraska to Minnesota. "Covered wagon" evokes images of *Little House on the Prairie,* but it had to have been a lot that way; in fact, my grandmother's passage was only a few years after the Laura Ingalls Wilder family adventures and remarkably close in miles to Walnut Grove, Minnesota, the setting of one of Wilder's sequels, *On the Banks of Plum Creek.*

The Bowen family stopped for two days, my mother says, in order for Grandma Bowen (my great-grandmother) to recover from the birth. When I was young and heard that story, an adult made a joke about the rocking of the wagon and "Grandma Bowen's buttermilk," a reference which I did not understand at the time but knew to be slightly untoward. However, my grandmother's birth *in medias res* did not seem to hold her back. She was one of seven lively sisters and one brother, Uncle Cliff, a friendly, cheerful man. Most photographs of my grandmother with her sisters show them turning toward each other, sometimes arranging one another's hair; often they are laughing. They were talkers in the best sense—willing to say what came into their heads, quick with their affection—and while they were deferential to their husbands, they were not cowed by them.

My grandmother took great pride in her flock of Rhode Island Red chickens, which had the auburn hues of her hair (it was orange fading to white when I was small). My grandfather always had a collie to bring home the dairy cows from the pasture. One time, after yet another incident with a bad collie and a dead chicken, she remarked to me, just out of earshot of my grandpa: "Buddy boy, I believe all the good dogs are dead."

She had not planned to marry. After her family settled in west-central Minnesota near Vining (her father worked on the railroad that unwound westward into North Dakota), she worked as a schoolteacher. There is a photo of her in school dress (long dark skirt, leather eyelet shoes, long-sleeved white blouse buttoned to a bow tie at her throat); beside her in a smiling row are nine children, as irregular in height as wildflowers. The girls are dressed in aprons over skirts, the boys in bib overalls and farm boots. Behind them is the school; the lower part of the belfry is in view. But my grandmother soon heard a higher calling: two traveling preachers came to the area, and she and some other young women began to attend Bible meetings. Soon she "professed," that is, joined the same Faith that my grandfather had cleaved to. This nondenominational religion had roots in England and Scotland, a kind of breakaway Protestantism that spoke to Bible-believing, mostly rural people. There is no church—meetings take place in the home—which allows the Faith to live and flourish under the big noses of the Lutheran and Catholic churches. The ethos is much about "blending and bending": living humbly, turning the other cheek, avoiding the sins of the world, and being helpful to others without making a big fuss about it. My mother has been a lifelong member except for a fallen stretch in her teens, and though the Faith tends to be pessimistic about the state of this world, her quick wit and humor have survived.

My grandmother's life in the "Work"—for a while she was one of the traveling preachers—required her to have no earthly possessions, board with "the flock," and remain single and celibate. Early on in her missionary work, however, she had health problems: diphtheria and some issue with blood clots in her legs. She was sent to recuperate on the Henry Miller farm in North Dakota, where Mrs. Miller, a nurse by training and a "refined woman" (my mother said there was always a fine white cloth on the dining room table), needed domestic help. Mrs. Miller had, after all, all those "grain boys" to feed.

I do not know the circumstances of their meeting—whether the moment when they first laid eyes on each other was a lightning bolt or only a shiver in their hearts—but Sarah Ella Bowen left the ministry for Oscar Sigurd Swenson. They were married in 1919. At first they sharecropped in North Dakota, but they had hard times during drought years and eventually crossed over to Becker County in north-central Minnesota. There was a period when they rented a farm in the fertile Red River Valley near Oslo, Minnesota, but in some manner my grandfather "lost" that arrangement; by inference, I believe he was outmaneuvered by a more aggressive neighboring farmer.

While my grandfather Swenson was a quiet, passive man, he was not lazy. When my mother was a little girl, every winter day except Sundays he went by horse and wagon to the woods where he cut pulp to supplement the farm income. There is a black-and-white photo of snowy forest and a tall, long rick of spruce logs—at least two train carloads—that he has cut with a Swede saw and piled by hand. No one today can imagine that amount of work. It is why my grandfather had thicker fingers than those of any man's hand I've ever held; they were cool to the touch, as if their blood flow had been beaten by unending work far below the surface of his lily-pad fingertips. Oscar Swenson was a man who in his lifetime "forked no lightning," as Dylan Thomas wrote near the end of his own father's life. But Oscar's steady approach to farm work and family life earned him the deep respect of everyone who knew him—including my father, who never fully understood why a man would not hunt, or go to war and not carry a rifle.

Chapter Two

As she grew into her teens, my mother chafed under life on the farm and especially under her parents' religion. The quiet Sundays. The mile, usually walked or skied, to country school. The thirty-mile trip (one way) from the farm to town. The dearth of neighbor girls with whom to socialize. She admits to being "especially rebellious" as a teenager, which I interpret as small acts of insurrection: not being timely in her chores, disappearing for long walks, being purposefully inattentive at Sunday morning church meetings. At age fifteen, however, she fell away from the Faith, and with her basket of naturally curly, slightly red-tinted hair she went off to Detroit Lakes, where she boarded during the week and attended high school. She came home only on weekends—weather permitting. In the summer, however, it was back to the farm. To the lazy cluck of the red chickens. The endless rows of garden peas. The buzz of cicadas. The flat, silent grainfields shimmering in the heat. A narrow gravel road ran north and south past the farm, and the dust of an approaching vehicle was a matter of interest even if the car or truck passed by, which most did. But not all. A book critic once wrote that much of literature falls into a simple plot: "And then a stranger came along."

The Weaver family's even-handed English name belied its personality. They were loud, argumentative Germans (Kuefner on my great-grandmother's side), with roots in Munich, a family washed west by the Johnstown, Pennsylvania, flood in the spring of 1889. They were working class, with houses that smelled of sauerkraut, but after landing in the Midwest the boys—my grandfather, Moffet, and his brothers—took to the outdoors with a vengeance. No more sidewalks. No more smoky city air. Unending opportunities to tramp the fields and groves with a shotgun in hand. While one branch of the Weaver family cleaved to Des Moines, Iowa, my grandfather headed farther west to the open country of Chamberlain, South Dakota, where he started a ranch. The true West was still open, but land was cheap in South Dakota, and game was abundant: pheasants, prairie chickens, geese, ducks, antelope, and deer. Hunting brought meat to the family table—was necessary work—but it is clear that my grandfather found roaming the land with a shotgun over his shoulder preferable to hoisting a fork or a shovel.

He was a true hunter, a crack shot. My father remembered stories of "three prairie chickens falling" from a single volley (for most hunters a double is good shooting). I cannot confirm this but heard more than once that my grandfather had an opportunity to go on the road with Winchester Repeating Arms Company, as it was called back then, as a demonstration shooter. One of those men who could dust five clay pigeons before they hit the ground. Who could powder a straight-away disk backwards over his shoulder. If the Winchester job offer was a true story, he probably turned it down because it would have taken him away from actual hunting.

I have his shotgun, a silvery Winchester Model 1912 twelve gauge. It is a slide-action, or "pump," nickel steel with an auburn-colored walnut stock and ribbed forearm grip. The serial number is 51836, low enough in one of the most popular shotgun series ever made to make gun collectors sit up and pay attention. I hunt with it on special occasions or when I feel the need to call up my father and granddad; usually in autumn I take it out once or twice if only to work its action and to make sure there are no rust spots inside the glowing, well-worn barrel.

A few years ago, during the construction of my house on the Mississippi River near Bemidji, the tradesmen were taking their afternoon coffee break. It was September, hunting season was approaching, and I was home to check on their progress. (If you are building a house anywhere in out-state Minnesota, make sure it is closed in—that is, windowed and roofed—before the leaves fall.) All that autumn their conversation had been about hunting and guns and shots they had made.

"So, do you hunt at all?" one of the carpenters asked, glancing at my khaki slacks, my dress shirt. My teaching clothes.

"Not as much as I used to," I said, and let it go at that.

The next time I came out to the house at coffee time I brought my grandfather's Winchester Model 12. After quickly and voluntarily wiping their hands on their Carhartts, the fellows passed around the gun with murmurs and nods as if handling a silver chalice of bird hunting. There is a short story by the Russian writer Isaac Babel called "My First Goose." It is set in wartime, and the narrator is an educated journalist-soldier thrown in among a unit of burly Cossacks.

The journalist feels he must prove himself and so kills an old lady's goose and makes her cook it for the men—who are duly impressed. Maybe that is what I was doing with the shotgun; afterward, the carpenters treated me differently— as if I might be, in the end, one of them.

My great-grandfather Ephraim B. Weaver fought in the Civil War. He enlisted with the Iowa 23rd Infantry in February of 1864. The only surviving words from his mouth about the war, passed through my grandfather and father, were that "blood ran in the streets." He might have been referring to the Battle of Vicksburg; however, that doesn't square with his enlistment date. Whether he meant combat at Black River, or Jackson, Mississippi, or Mobile, Alabama, he escaped gunshot wounds and disease but when he came home after the war he was "unable to do much," as my father described it—a phrase accepted by everyone as easily as if he had returned with a missing leg or arm. There is always a new term for mental disability brought on by war. It was "shell shock" during the First and Second World Wars; the clumsy "post-traumatic stress syndrome," or PTSD, for the Vietnam War; but the Civil War commands the most poetic and metaphorical of descriptions: "soldier's heart." There is a grainy black-and-white photo of Ephraim Weaver as an old man. It is winter, and he stands straightly with his axe beside tidy ricks of carefully split and stacked firewood. "That's pretty much all he did," my father explained of his grandfather—"make firewood for us."

For my grandfather Moffet Weaver, South Dakota was too hot and dry. There are fragments of stories about the cistern, which was always low, and its foul-smelling water. In 1914 he packed up his family and came to northern Minnesota, a region with more than enough trees and fresh water.

He homesteaded on the east side of Sweitzer Lake in central Hubbard County; the county seat, Park Rapids, had four hundred lakes within a twenty-mile radius. With four growing sons and one daughter to help out on the farm, he could now fish and hunt until the cows came home—actually, until well after the cows came home.

Neither was my grandfather Weaver a lazy man, but he was not big on milking cows or doing barn chores (along with the dairy there was a good-sized chicken-and-egg operation); that kind of work he turned over to his family. During the summer harvest season he went on the road doing custom grain harvesting. Most smaller farms could not afford to own a grain thresher for one week's use and were happy to pay a traveling crew to show up and do the dusty, dangerous work of running a Hart-Parr or similar steam engine with its long, whirring, "endless" drive-belt that connected to an elephant-sized, roaring threshing machine. It took men with confidence, with wanderlust, to pull the big, iron-wheeled equipment across the counties. And the arrival of the threshing convoy, like a circus coming up the road complete with a long toot and shriek of a steam whistle, was a great relief to a farmer waiting with one eye on the weather and the other on his fields of wheat, oats, or barley. For farm children—and for a young woman such as my mother— the arrival of "the men" had to have been a source of great excitement.

I would like to say that my mother met my father during the harvest season. That the Weaver threshing crew came to the Swenson farm, and that she was delivering water to the men in the field on a hot August day and saw him—or he her. Their eyes locked. A lightning bolt. That story easily could have occurred. My father did indeed help thresh grain on the Swenson farm, but somehow he and my mother did not meet there or learn anything about one another. Still, the two families were bridged by the grain harvest, which gave my mother and father something in common when they met a year or so later in Park Rapids, where she boarded during her senior year in high school.

My father was older by seven years, which put their dating on the fringe of appropriateness (she was eighteen, he was twenty-five). They soon married but did not have their first child, my sister Connie, until four years later. During that space of time, my mother believed, increasingly, that she was being punished by God for her wildness. She told my sisters this. I also believe that is the reason my mother returned, at age twenty-four, to her parents' religion—an act which caught my father off guard. Initially he must have been bewildered. But that confusion devolved to a sense of betrayal and then to anger that he carried into middle age and that had a corrosive effect upon their marriage and our family life.

When I was young, he was particularly agitated by the "two-by-two" preachers who came for brief stays at our house (even as a very young boy I got the feeling that they stayed longer at other people's homes). While polite to the pairs of Sisters, he was openly scornful, even hostile, to the Brothers. They were pale, indoor kind of men who saw their labors confined to the spiritual realm; at the most, their contribution for bed and board was to peel potatoes or husk sweet corn for supper, prior to which one of them gave an interminable blessing. During grace my father would not bow his head or close his eyes. I know this because he kept a steely gaze upon me as if to make sure I was not falling, hook, line, and sinker, for this God-will-provide bullshit.

His anger simmered over the years and occasionally boiled over. Once, raging, he told my mother that he doubted I was his son—that I probably belonged to "one of those damn preachers." My mother told me this herself. Eventually, late in life and plagued by health issues, my father accepted Jesus Christ but "struggled" with that decision, as my mother described it, until the end. His was not a deathbed conversion, but it came late enough—in his seventies—to feel like a compromise of some kind. By then he was increasingly dependent on my mother and home health aides for his daily care, and perhaps he found himself in a corner, his sharp edges worn down by unceasing kindnesses. Surrounded by charity and goodness. The fight gone out of him. In the end, his conversion might have been more of a gesture to his caregivers than a spiritual transformation, but I missed the lean, sun-browned, hawk-eyed man he used to be.

Chapter Three

There was never any question that I would be a hunter. My first gun was the end of a curved, wooden barn rafter that I sawed to fit my skinny arms, then painted the yellow pine wood a gunmetal gray with red accents for the imaginary trigger. A small block of wood became the fore-arm grip; secured with a small nail, the grip rotated and gave the gun the sense of a moving "action." The muzzle end was drilled out as deep as a boy's pinky finger in order to replicate the open bore of a real barrel. Its front sight was the hoop of a small, wire staple. Eighteen inches behind the sight was the real action—a squeeze-type wooden clothes-pin. Glued atop the barrel, the clothespin was my trigger release for rubber bands. The firing sequence was simple: loop rubber band onto front sight, stretch back to clothespin, clamp, aim, fire. My rubber-band rifle was ingenious and effective. More than once I stung my sisters with it—and got chased and spanked for my bad behavior.

But my cousin Gerry and I, along with our neighbors the Williams boys, had always played "shoot" games of various kinds. These included cowboys and Indians as well as "Germans." The latter involved "grenades," which we made from corncobs and chicken feathers. Take one shelled cob; find three White Rock (or equivalent) chicken feathers of equal size; insert their vanes into the soft, pale core of the butt end of the cob; twist the feathers slightly outward in a spiral pattern so that the cob will rotate when lobbed (a well-constructed corncob grenade should fly with a rifling effect). Our game of grenades was always more about flight performance than accuracy. However, when the missile was launched the intended target had to freeze. No dodging. No running. A hit, of course, meant death.

From rubber-band rifles we worked our way upward to slingshots. These we made from the forks of box elder branches: find a branch about thumb thick with a perfect Y fork; cut to size for comfort in your hand; peel and lightly notch the top of each fork; cut two thin strips of inner-tube rubber; from tanned deer hide, cut an egg-sized oval of soft buckskin (this will be the pocket, or cup, between the rubber bands). Make a small slit just inside the edges of the pocket. Insert ends of tire rubber into buckskin slits, fold, stretch, and tie with fishing line (this requires four small to medium-sized hands). Attach catapult rubber bands, one each, to the notched, upper forks with fishing line (use four hands, as above). Be sure to stretch the rubber band tightly before tying the fine line as close as possible to the wood. This is a crucial step: an improperly tied rubber band on a finished slingshot will, at full draw, let loose and slap your face as it has not been slapped before.

We ranged freely with our slingshots and were always on the lookout for the perfect stone—smooth, a little bigger than a marble, and with some weight to it (not all stones have the same specific gravity). We were good shots. Good enough to knock a pigeon off the ridge roll of a dairy barn. Pigeons were dirty birds—hard to keep out of the hayloft, where they shit on the hay bales—and, along with sparrows, my first true targets. Slingshot stones were not good in the hayloft (they could break a light bulb), so my weapon of choice was a bow and arrow. It was a single-curve, wooden longbow. The two ends were bent toward each other and strung tautly with a window shade cord that more than once peeled a patch of skin off the inside of my forearm. Late summer was the best time to hunt pigeons in the loft; the mountain of sweet-smelling new hay bales reached two-thirds of the way to the rafters of the cavernous room, and their green, stubbly sides made a staircase for climbing. Pigeons, not totally dumb, fluttered off at first sight of a boy with a bow and arrow, but the end game was patience. I hid myself among the bales and waited for their return. It sometimes took an hour or more, but eventually pigeon claws scraped atop the tin ridge roll, and soon enough the birds fluttered back inside to their nests high up on the back wall. If alone, I had time for one good shot. With Gerry, we employed another tactic: we waited, then bolted out, shouting and waving our arms. The frightened pigeons often forgot their way out of the loft, and we then had our personal shooting gallery. As the frantic birds fluttered back and forth we shot again and again (our wooden arrows were too dull to lodge in the wooden rafters). Finally, exhausted, the blue and gray birds sat for a killing blow.

English sparrows in the granary were also fair game. The problem lay not in the grain they ate, but their droppings that fell into it—black seeds of shit mixing with the oats, which were a staple feed for the dairy cows. Sparrows received no quarter. The granary was the old-school kind, tall and square with a rectangular commons area just inside and high wooden bins around. Each bin had removable slide boards on its inside face and a small, shutter-type door on the exterior wall through which we shoveled grain and, later, pumped in grain with an electric auger. Our granary had an upstairs loft with wooden steps leading to it. The steps swung upward on a pulley; if need be, they could be hoisted out of the way, but I preferred them down, which allowed me to sneak up the stairs and ambush a flock of sparrows.

Hunting was in closer quarters in the granary loft, which was cluttered with relics: old steamer trunks, horse tack, a kraut cutter, a cream separator, a butter churn, a couple of crank-type phones that were (for littler kids) fun to play with, except that the boxy old phones and most things in the loft were spotted with sparrow guano. The loft had a barn window, about two feet square with a small, four-paned sash, on either end of the chamber; the frightened sparrows always mistook the glowing dusty windows for their escape routes. For sky. They fluttered side to side, thudding into the glass.

Sometimes, when there was a particularly bad infestation of sparrows, Gerry and I teamed up. One of us kept the birds flying back and forth, while the other stood in the middle of the loft and flailed at them with a badminton racquet or baseball bat. Usually one or more of the big male barn cats lurked nearby, snatching up "singles" and "doubles" (crippled birds). Afterward, when the sparrows were either all dead or escaped down the stairwell, we bagged the dead ones— carefully, because both sparrows and pigeons had fleas—and took them to the hayloft for the mother cats, who, with kittens to guard against old tomcats, could not easily get out to hunt.

Most boys in the 1950s went through a Roy Rogers stage (I still have my tin Roy Rogers lunch box), which required chaps, a white, felt cowboy hat—and especially a BB gun. The BB gun was the natural evolutionary step forward in weaponry and was needed to fend off cattle rustlers, marauding Comanches, and varmints of all kinds, including stagecoach bandits. Those being in short supply, I turned my aim on English sparrows and red squirrels. The little air gun was hardly strong enough to kill anything but still could spiderweb a hayloft window or sting a pigeon.

My first real gun was a single-shot .22 rifle acquired with S & H Green Stamps. In the 1960s, green stamps were collected by 80 percent of shoppers—including my mother—then pasted into booklets. When the booklets were filled, their pages thickened from the licked stamps and the glue that tasted like white paste, we took them to an S & H redemption center, a small catalog store in town. S & H catalogs offered everything from dishware to sporting goods, and if an item was not in the catalog, it paid to ask. I do not remember how many books my rifle required, but certainly a serious amount—likely a couple of years' worth of licking and pasting. I was around ten years old when we secured the rifle; I had to pass a gun safety course in order to get my first deer license at age thirteen, but I'm certain I had the .22 well before that. I remember my father showing me how to shoot the little rifle (a bolt action)—and reminding me that it was not a toy.

I nodded eagerly.

"Remember what happened to Kenny Nasser," my father added.

But that was a deer rifle! Luckily I didn't say those words, which probably would have kept me from my gun for another year. A .22 rifle could also kill a person.

The Nasser family lived on a farm a mile south; the Larsons, a hardscrabble farm family, lived a mile to the northeast—which is to say that both families were close neighbors. Kenny Nasser was a lively, bright, fair-haired, seven-year-old boy, my age. Leonard Larson was a jug-eared, reddish-haired retarded kid, older, a lot stronger, piss-smelly, and slightly out of control (he did not go to school); he had to be watched because he was so rough on us younger kids. It happened in November, just after deer season, at the Larson house. Someone had not put away the hunting rifle. The boys were playing. No one really knows what happened (I was not there), but Leonard aimed and shot Kenny dead with a .30–30.

The funeral was the saddest thing to happen in my life thus far. I could not look up from my good shoes. My eyes dripped tears and left spots on their polished brown leather. I do not remember if the Larson family attended—I doubt it. But as my father held out the shiny, new, bolt-action .22 rifle, I nodded my head and murmured, "I remember."

With that, the gun was mine. During the next couple of summers, when I was too young to drive a tractor and too skinny to buck bales, the little rifle was always on my shoulder. My first useful targets were gophers, which came in two varieties. Pocket gophers were the size of brown rats but swam underground like miniature beavers. With the same curving front teeth and serious front claws for digging, they unwound necklace chains of dirt mounds across the hayfields as they chewed off the roots of alfalfa and clover. The hummocks of excavated earth jolted the tractor and wrecked cutting sickles on hay mowers and swathers. The township board offered a twenty-five-cent bounty for each gopher (my father chipped in another dime), which required proof of purchase—in this case, the severed front claws. But first I had to catch the little rodents.

I worked: from mound, estimate the direction of tunnel to next mound. Probe ground with thin metal rod to find tunnel. Excavate just enough to insert either leg-hold, pan-type trap or the improved, wire-spring "Death Clutch" brand. Stake trap in place so the gopher will not drag it backward out of reach; move on to next set; return to field next morning. Some traps will be plugged tight with dirt and that particular gopher difficult to catch the next time (a catch-to-plugged ratio of 2-for-3 was good). Remove dead gophers from successful sets. Nip off front feet with jackknife or light hatchet. I always carried a small plastic bag for gopher feet; the little claws were sharp, however, and often poked through both plastic and pocket to scratch the outside of my thigh. Trapping pocket gophers was an art and science, and it took much of one summer to learn the trade, but after that I made good money.

My sister Connie also trapped gophers. Once she tried to double dip on her gopher bounty; after catching a very pregnant gopher, she slit open the belly, removed the babies, snipped off their feet too, and tried to pass them by my father. He was not amused.

Gopher claws we kept in a sealed tin can with nail punctures for air, but one had to be careful about flies and maggots; it was better to keep them in the freezer until it was time to redeem them at a township board meeting. There a board member, usually an old farmer, counted them in pairs on a newspaper, using a stick or ruler to move the dried claws like a pharmacist counting pills. I counted with him, moving my lips, eager for my cash. During my heyday of gopher trapping, I ran a line of twenty or so traps and made five dollars a day.

However, when a pocket gopher was removed from this earth, another kind moved in, the thirteen-lined ground squirrel or "striped gophers," as we called them. A smaller version of a prairie dog, these gophers took over the vacant tunnels and brought their own problems—especially to farmers with livestock. Ground squirrels maintained open holes, which became ankle turners for cows and horses. My job, then, was to take my .22 and shoot the striped gophers. Atop the ground they were quick-moving and always alert—with a weather eye for red-tailed hawks—but after scurrying into a hole, most every striped gopher could not resist lifting his head above ground for one more look. The best and steadiest shooting angle was fully prone, a position that often coaxed the gopher to raise his head and little brown eyes just a tad higher. Take one more peek.

In this way, sun-cured and carefree, I spent my summers ranging the fields and woods. There were close to one thousand acres of Weaver land. My father's and my uncles' farms were contiguous to my grandfather's, and all of it was open to me. I often took my lunch and sometimes had a short nap in a sunny spot and then moved on. I was "green and golden," as Dylan Thomas wrote about his youth. But one summer afternoon, heading home from the hill, I stopped by my cousin's farm. Gerry was around, and we ended up hanging out in his father's garage where my uncle Jim had some World War II memorabilia. He had been in the "thick of it" (the only thing he ever said about the war), including the Normandy invasion, and had brought home a German helmet. I was examining the helmet just as Uncle Jim walked in. I turned to him with great enthusiasm and asked, "How many Germans did you kill?"

He got an odd, slightly stricken look on his face. "You don't really ask a man that kind of question," he said. He took the helmet from my hands and hung it back on the wall. I had never seen that kind of look before on anyone's face; I felt ashamed of myself for causing it.

"You boys go outside and play," he said gruffly.

Gerry and I did, but the day was not the same. I walked home soon after that with my little .22 rifle over my shoulder. I also carried a vague but gloomy feeling that something large had changed in my life, and that there was no changing it back.

Chapter Four

The possibility of shooting accidents are part of the territory of gun ownership. However, for people who grow up with guns and know how to use them, the chance of a shooting accident is on the order of drawing a royal flush in a poker game.

Which happens.

When I was eight or nine, I was snooping in the bottom of my father's little red-cedar handkerchief box, where I found a small, misshapen slug. It looked like a squashed cricket. The flattest side of the lead had a fine, thread-like pattern. Curiosity ruled, and I took it to my father.

My father looked up (he was working or reading the newspaper—doing something). He squinted. "That's a .22 slug," he said. "Your uncle Emery shot me in the knee with it. Not his fault, though—it ricocheted off the railroad tracks."

I held the slug closer to my eyes.

"You can see the pattern of my pants in the lead," he said.

It was true—the tiny weave of threads. "Did it hurt?"

"Not that bad," my father said, returning to his business at hand. "Though he had to carry me home, and then we both got a whipping before we went to town. Dr. Higgs took it out. It was stuck under my kneecap."

I would guess that he also got a whipping for the time his own .22 rifle went off in the house. The bullet hit the glass eye of a taxidermy deer head hung high on the wall, then glanced across the room, narrowly missing my grandmother. Boys playing with guns. The old, twice-shot buck hangs in the mudroom of my house, banished there by my wife, who has set an upper limit of deer heads (two) in our living room and who finds the one-eyed deer slightly creepy. I have found it useful to show to small boys wild to shoot guns and kill things: the blank eye always gets their attention.

My second cousin David was less fortunate than my father. David's gun accident involved a shotgun that slid off a tractor he was driving; the gun detonated and blew a hole in his side. The shotgun was a .410, the smallest bore, with shells about the size of a man's pinky finger. David had loaded his gun with light bird load, or "fine shot," which in the end might have worked against him; a single bullet, his doctor said, is always easier to deal with.

Everette Duthoy, MD, is a silver-haired, soft-spoken man, a doctor's doctor, now retired. He did various stitchings on me when I was a boy, and in our small town we all knew him well. After speaking with David, I wrote Dr. Duthoy about the mishap and what he remembered—what, professionally speaking, he could tell me.

He quickly got in touch. "What do I remember about Dave's accident?" he replied by letter. "Well, just about everything. Those kinds of cases do not come along often in the practice of a country doctor. Thank goodness."

He wrote about David's "acute belly, indicating peritonitis and ruptured internal organs." How he operated as soon as an anesthetist could be found and worked on the "lacerated right kidney, penetrating wounds of the liver and diaphragm with multiple foreign bodies impregnating the liver and abdomen." How there were bile and blood filling the abdominal cavity, and how he had to remove clothing and other foreign bodies from the wound, stop the bleeding, and repair the holes in the diaphragm, liver, and kidney, "which was no small task for a small town GP surgeon." How it was lucky that Dave was young and healthy to begin with, because post-op he had a stomach tube, antibiotics, and IVs, and ten days later a sudden high fever from an infection. "He lost about 30 pounds," Dr. Duthoy wrote, "and was hospitalized for a month. Our bill for the surgeries and hospital care was $350. His mother came to the office to thank me and write a check for the total amount. I thanked her and stated that I lost a lot of sleep worrying about Dave."

And then there was my great-uncle. Below is his obituary, which I include here both for its cautionary tale (fences and guns) and for its clear, hymn-like writing.

Shoots Self Accidentally

Will Weaver Received a Fatal Wound and
Lived Only a Short Time

Wm. H. Weaver accidentally shot himself with a shot gun Wednesday afternoon and lived only a short time after the accident. The full particulars of how it happened are not known as no one witnessed the accident and the victim did not explain it.

Mr. Weaver had started over to the home of his brother, O. O. Weaver, for some milk and was taking his shot gun, which was a twelve gauge Remington hammerless pump gun, along to shoot any game that he might see. He had gone to a calf pasture about 200 rods from the house and it is presumed that in climbing over the fence, which was too tight for him to go through, his gun was in some manner discharged. The charge entered the victim's body below the ribs on the left side, passing through the right lung and lodging in the right shoulder.

Notwithstanding the fatal wound and the loss of blood Mr. Weaver was able to walk to the house more than half a mile away. Upon reaching home he informed his wife that he had shot himself and told her to send for a doctor. She hurried to the Fred Sellner home and Fred went on to John Crabtree's and the two came to town for Dr. Kimble. Mrs. Weaver returned home and found her husband lying on his face, very weak from loss of blood. He was still conscious and able to talk when Dr. Kimble arrived, the doctor having made a quick run in the Shoemaker auto. It was evident at a glance that the wound was a very serious one, if not fatal, so Dr. Williamson was sent for for a consultation, but he being out of town Dr. Hunt, of Draper, was phoned for and he came over in an auto. He arrived at about seven o'clock, and Dr. Williamson soon after, but the wounded man had passed away at 4:30.

The accident was a sad one and is another example of the uncertainty of life. "In life we are in death."

Des Moines Register, 1911

I have had two close calls with shooting mishaps. The first scared me but was not serious. Rose, my new wife, and I were living in California at the time and made a trip up to Montana to see a friend, Jack, from college. It was October. I had missed the hunting in Minnesota, and so we were hunting grouse in a Montana river bottom. Rose, the good sport and observer. Me. Jack. Jack's brother, Marty, who had a couple of friends with him. Too many people already. The birds were in very dense alders (grouse eat the buds, and the mesh of branches protects the birds from owls). A brace of partridge exploded upward. Someone fired—and then again. Fine shot whacked around us like an attack of hornets—one of which stung my forearm. I shouted, and the shooting stopped. One bird was down, and afterward we somewhat sheepishly reconvened on the trail to make sure everyone was all right. Rose was not a hunter, and I tried to make light of the incident, but it should not have happened.

The second mishap predated her and shook my whole family. It happened during deer season on a day when, against my father's better judgment, one of my uncles had invited the new Lutheran preacher to hunt with us. I remember (I think I was in junior high) that the man was slightly loud and overly cheerful; he had on new, red hunting clothes (this was before the mandatory blaze orange) and too many of them. If he had to walk anywhere, he would have overheated after fifty yards. He also seemed slightly careless with his rifle, which carried a large telescopic sight (not much use in our style of hunting). Gun safety starts and ends with muzzle control: if the end of a barrel never swings toward someone, no one will ever get shot. However, the preacher had what I call "wandering barrel" syndrome—enough to make me step back and to the side as we stood around in the snow and planned the drive.

Our hunting party was all Weavers except for some of the Williams family, whose land adjoined ours to the north. We all knew the drill. Some posted themselves on stands while others (usually the younger ones) beat the brush and tried to push the deer toward the waiting guns. That day, the question quickly became what to do with the preacher.

The hosting uncle prevailed in getting the preacher a prime stand near the cornfield, beyond which was the woods. "Goddamnit, he'll get lost otherwise," Uncle Emery said, while the preacher looked on, a smile pasted on his face. (My father and uncles were public arguers; they never cared who listened.)

My cousin Gerry and I were resigned to being drivers, which is to say, walkers. Brush-pounders. Woods-beaters. Younger hunters had to earn their way—an implicit apprentice system—to "stander" status, but I was gun-shy in my bones about the preacher and not unhappy to head into the woods, where we spread out. Drives are hard and often fruitless work, but not long into this one, one of the pushers called, "There they go!"

Two deer, white flags up, bounded forward out of sight; none of us shot because none of us had a good shot and, besides, our fathers (and the preacher) were less than one hundred yards ahead. They would get the good shots. We waited, but none of their rifles barked in the cold November air.

In the brush, we signaled each other up and down the line: move forward again. A few minutes later we reached the edge of the woods and the beginning of cornfield; across were the red coats of the standers. One of the uncles beckoned us forward, into the cornfield.

"Stay low and don't shoot no matter what," I whispered to Gerry as we entered the tall corn. The pale yellow, frozen fronds were sharp on the face. We eased forward down the rows, unable to see anything but corn. The tension rose. The deer were most certainly still in the cornfield.

Suddenly there was thrashing ahead, then shouting—the deer had bolted forward—then an impossibly loud blast.

A rifle report close at hand is at first only concussion.

Air movement. Lightning beside you—things seem to split and explode—and only then comes the thunder. My ears rang as I dove to the ground. The blasting continued—perhaps four shots total. It only stopped when men shouted, then screamed for a halt. It was the preacher: he had shot into the cornfield, straight down the rows.

There was silence, then a call out to see if we were all right (we were), then so much swearing—I could hear my father's voice leading the charge—that Gerry and I lingered in the cornfield, out of sight. When we finally emerged, the preacher was heading briskly across the field toward his truck. My father walked behind him and then stopped, jaw set, to watch him leave—as if to make sure he vacated the premises.

Afterward, in a rare moment, one of my uncles kicked at the snow. "Goddamnit," he said, "I thought he would know how to hunt!" It was as close to an apology as I ever heard between the adult brothers.

My father could only shake his head. He let out a long breath, then said, "I think we're done hunting for today."

Gerry and I looked at each other with disbelief: it was only two o'clock in the afternoon! But we followed our fathers to their pickups and went home. My father had to explain to my mother why we were in from the field so early; she was not happy with any part of our story. He and I kept a very low profile the rest of the afternoon—which felt oddly like Sunday. We played checkers, and that night at supper I noticed another odd thing. During my mother's blessing of the food I thought I saw my father, ever so slightly, bow his head.

Chapter Five

My father, Harold, was born in 1913, and the summer he was eleven his life took an unlucky turn. It was August and he was doing a man's work, kicking colter on the breaking plow. A breaking plow turns virgin soil, in this case, northern Minnesota cutover land. The big iron implement looks like a giant grasshopper with a sharp, drooping beak. Tractor-drawn thrust gathers below grade in a single, oversized, curved plowshare led by a heavy-duty horizontal knife (or "lay"); a colter is a cutting disk that slices the earth ahead of the plowshare. Even though the pine trees had been cut and their stumps pulled out—the most stubborn were dynamited—a mess of gnarly roots and snags remained in the ground. My father's job, then, was to walk close alongside the plow and kick away the tangle of woody debris that rose up between the colter and plowshare.

But on that hot summer day of 1924 it was not a farm accident but an odd feeling—chills and a sudden fever—that sent him home sick. He went to bed and the next day could not get up. His condition persisted until a doctor came to the house a couple of days later and gave the verdict: polio.

My father's case contradicted theories of the time—that polio was a communicable disease of large cities and was caught in crowded public places such as swimming pools and schools. But none of that mattered: he, alone among his five siblings, had it. In fact, only one other boy in the whole county, Irwin Auer, contracted polio. There would be more waves of polio, especially in the 1930s and 1940s and until the Jonas Salk "sugar cube" vaccine arrived in 1954, but my father's case was the first in our northern Minnesota county.

He was immobilized in bed from August until December, when a place finally opened at the Gillette Children's Hospital in St. Paul. Within bad luck there can be a measure of good luck; his was Gillette Hospital and Sister Kenny. A nurse (not a nun) who lived in New South Wales and did not come to America until 1940, Sister Kenny employed controversial theories on the treatment of infantile paralysis that had preceded her all the way to Minnesota. Prior to Sister Kenny, the treatment for polio included splints, casts, and immobilization of the patient—a course of action perhaps worse, in the end, than doing nothing—on the order of bleeding a patient to make him stronger. Sister Kenny believed in aggressive physical therapy—massage, movement, anything to keep the muscles from atrophying. My father believed that immobilization is what caused the damage during his four-month wait for a bed at Gillette.

My father spent a full year in Gillette Children's Hospital, which was almost exactly two hundred miles from home in northern Minnesota. During that time, none of his family came to see him. It was, after all, 1925. Distances were longer then. The trip would have taken most of the day—and then an expensive motel of some kind—and then another day's travel to get back home. There was the livestock. The chickens. The garden. And of course the hunting and fishing.

He did receive one visit from people he knew. A family from Hubbard County by the name of Rixen came to the hospital to see a relative and also took time to see my father. They reported back on "Willie" (my father's nickname)— that afterward he followed them out on his crutches and hid nearby, eavesdropping for any news of home.

If none of his family came to visit him, Babe Ruth did. My father got his autograph, a cramped but legible signature, in a little, blue, hardback booklet. I ran across it years later, and my father told me the story of The Babe's visit: how he came to see the children. Ruth was a big man with giant hands, my father recalled. I was fascinated by the autograph and sometime along about seventh grade made the mistake of sneaking it off to school to impress my friends. Somehow, something happened to it; I might have traded the autograph away or in some manner was talked out of it. How it was lost I cannot recall, and it is probably better that way.

My father returned home in the winter of 1926 a "cripple," but in word only. His polio had left him with a withered left leg and weakened arm, but he was mobile, though with a limp. Undoubtedly he felt lucky to walk out of Gillette; certainly there were many children who did not, and who spent the rest of their lives in wheelchairs, and who eventually died from paralysis of the chest and diaphragm that left them unable to breathe. The so-called iron lung machine, invented to assist breathing, was not used until 1928.

Back home, he set about making up for lost time by fishing and hunting (and getting shot by his brother). In school he was a likeable troublemaker, quick to fight if he had to, and good at math. He eventually became, I believe, something of a lady's man. My mother met him when he showed up unexpectedly in Park Rapids with his older brother, Emery, having been "thrown over by some girl from Idaho," the particulars of which are not known.

There is a photo of my mother with her brother, Claron, and my father. Claron Swenson wears bib overalls; he is slim, open-faced, untroubled, fully in the moment. My father, wearing an open-collared jacket, is darker-haired, stronger in the chest and shoulders. He has his hands in his pockets, and he squints against the sun. He carries the sense of having been places and seen things; there is a hint of the dark side about him.

His polio also did not stop him from becoming a successful farmer and active citizen. For many years he was on the township board and also was a county fire warden (people dropped by for burning permits and often stayed for coffee) and county weed inspector. However, like a very slow cancer, his polio gradually claimed more and more of his physical and psychological life.

The first of the two is easier to chart. During my growing-up years on our farm he walked with a pronounced limp—a dipping motion to the left—and always took the shortest route between things: seats and perches to sit on, counters and benches to lean against. The chores, as in barn work, were difficult—shoveling in particular, an act that requires a lot of leg power. He could not run. We never played chase or yard ball or anything that involved agility and motion and speed.

My father's limitations in this area once worked to the benefit of my sister Connie. She was a wild child who got pregnant at age sixteen and married the father that same year.

I remember a scene (it might have been when she broke the news of her pregnancy): the kitchen table was between her and my father and he wanted to catch her—to do what? Slap her? Hit her? He was not that kind of father. But she was too quick for him, for his legs, and she darted right when he went left and left when he lurched right, and eventually she escaped out the front door and ran north to the windbreak, where her boyfriend was waiting, his hot rod hidden behind the trees.

My father's polio also affected the division of labor on the farm. Our dairy farm, as most were then, was built around a fork, a shovel, and a milk pail. All work was by hand. We eventually acquired a hired man, Carl, a small, wiry, slightly retarded fellow—but no fool—to help with barn duties. Carl handled the dairy herd, which included feeding, milking, and barn cleaning; my father focused on fieldwork, which allowed him to stay much of the time aboard a tractor or swather or combine. This left me, the only son, with more free time than most farm boys, a gift that shaped the direction of my life. Among farm boys I was privileged, thanks to Carl; I had time for after-school sports, for rambling in the woods with my shotgun, for reading, and for the beginning of a life of the mind.

But polio was a noose around my father's world. As he aged, the physical effects of it tightened their grip on mind and body. His limp worsened. He went from a walking stick in his fifties to crutches in his sixties to a wheelchair and an electric cart in his seventies. Besides shrinking his mobility, post-polio syndrome carried an array of subtler slings and arrows, including fibromyalgia and respiratory and circulatory problems. How could he not focus on his physical troubles at the expense of his spirit? Even when we children were young, when we took family outings to Itasca State Park or to the waterfalls by Lake Superior, his first thought must have been how to park the car close by. And were there handrails or at least something to hold on to? How far would he have to walk? Why would there not be a hard place—or, at the least, an occupied space—in his heart?

On the other hand, it is tricky sorting out what part of his hard-boiled nature came from his polio and what part came from his family life. The Weavers had always been tough on their own. His brothers cut him little slack about his handicap. All the Weavers were quick to judge, were Republican to the bone, and believed that nothing in life was free—no handouts, survival of the fittest, "root, hog, or die." My father blamed Democrats for most everything wrong with the world, right down to the laws requiring seat belts in cars. He believed, about car crashes, that it was not only a person's right but a far better thing to be thrown clear—and luckily he never had to test that theory because he never buckled a seat belt in his life.

Politics of the 1960s slowly colored our relationship, particularly during the Vietnam period. Two of his brothers, James and Curtis, had fought in World War II, and he most certainly would have also were it not for his disability. He believed in the domino theory, was dead set against Communists and liberals—though was not loud or public about his politics. The draft of the late 1960s and early 1970s must have made him think about me, his one son; if so, he never said anything.

The first national draft lottery was held on December 1, 1969, when I was a freshman at St. Cloud State College. The Stearns Hall dormitory held a pizza party for the event, in the game room on the first floor. Ping-pong tables were pushed aside, chairs arranged facing the single television, and gradually the room filled with young men until the space became close. Warm. We all tried to be nonchalant about the lottery, but as the witching hour approached the room gradually grew quiet.

The process of the lottery was fairly simple. The days of the year, from 1 to 366 (leap year was included), had been written on small slips of paper. Each was inserted in a plastic capsule the size of a lip balm tube. All 366 were put into a shoe box and shaken (not nearly enough, statisticians would later prove), then dumped into a large glass jar. From there they were withdrawn one at a time by a serious-faced man in a black suit, white shirt, and skinny black tie who looked like a science teacher; the whole process resembled some kind of crazy lab experiment.

The first number drawn was 257, which corresponded to September 14—which became the dreaded number 1. That is, young men with September 14 birthdays would be drafted first—and almost certainly sent to Vietnam. My birthday landed on number 58, also a dead man's draw. But there were other boys with lower numbers than mine, and the evening progressed with whoops of joy, or groans, or a deep sucking in of breath. By the end of the drawing the game room had become dizzyingly warm and rank with body odor. Death was all around.

After the lottery that night there was partying for real, but the event itself was a whiff of smelling salts. I had stumbled through my first quarter of college life, and there was more flailing to come as I took various classes in search of a major. But now life was serious. Decisions had to be made. I was already drawn to the antiwar movement—had mostly made up my mind about Vietnam—but I went home the weekend after the lottery to lick my wounds and think about things.

My father was not the kind of man to sit down and lay out life's various options—to talk things through. In fact, I think we went to his spear house on Sweitzer Lake and sat several hours in silence, staring through a square hole in the ice at our circling, red-and-white decoy. I do not remember if we speared a pike or not, but the warm, dark fish house was not the worst place to have deep thoughts.

Not long after that trip home I declared myself a conscientious objector. This required me to send a letter with my reasons to my local draft board in Hubbard County. Draft boards were nearly always a group of older men, the kind who had time on their hands (meaning, retired farmers and store owners) and who were by nature conservative. I recognized several of their names: august, stalwart citizens of our rural community. The same men who had once counted my gopher feet.

My letter—my case—took a risky line. While I might have used my mother's religion and my grandfather Swenson's history as a CO in World War I, I did not. It felt false and wrong because I did not subscribe to that religion. The only argument remaining was the "ethical appeal," which made more sense to me anyway. I wrote that I had met people from other countries and had studied history and foreign languages and that I considered myself a patriotic American but also a citizen of the world. I further wrote that while I had never backed down from a fight, neither had I ever hit another person with a closed fist, and that fighting—and wars—seldom solved things. I also wrote that, in part because I was a hunter, I did not think I could kill another man.

The letter was a fine mess, overwritten and overthought, but I sent it off. In the days that followed I expected to be summoned—called upon the carpet to answer such trick questions as, "What if a rapist broke into your house and came after your mother? Would you defend her? Would you defend yourself?" With the help of antiwar pamphlets from a Quaker group in Minneapolis I studied all the logical fallacies surrounding conscientious objection and was ready for my grilling. However, after an agonizing month of no response, an envelope came. Inside was the barest of letters stating that my application had been approved. Included was a new draft card with 1-O status for conscientious objection.

I did not whoop for joy or head out to party that night. It was not that kind of victory—there were no victories for anyone during the Vietnam War. My first act was to call home with the news. My mother's voice carried great relief, but she tried to be measured about it—which meant that my father was within earshot. "I'll tell your dad," she said.

I do not remember that he ever said anything specifically about my conscientious objector status, but the Vietnam War always simmered just below the surface. As campus protests heated to boiling, my father and I came to an unspoken agreement: we did not talk about Vietnam. Not even when young men from the county began to be killed there, including Gary Rehn, the only son of a family who lived a couple of miles east of our farm and whom we knew well from my sister Judy's class. Gary and all the others killed, in my mind then and now, for no good reason.

But I must have felt lost to my father, too. I grew my hair long and transferred to the University of Minnesota, main campus, to be at the center of things. There were invisible wisps of eye-biting tear gas in the great reading room of Walter Library, helicopters passing *whak-whak-whak* overhead, giant barricades, and bonfires of trash and wooden pallets on University Avenue. Senator Eugene McCarthy came to speak to thousands gathered on the main mall, and afterward the Minneapolis police "tactical squad," black visors down and name tags taped over, cleared the streets with the marching movement of clumsy fencers—step and thrust, step and thrust—until they could no longer restrain themselves, broke ranks, and chased students across the tree-lined mall and against fences and into corners, where they beat them with their black batons.

In the summer of 1972, after the protests had peaked and done their work (Nixon was trying to find "peace with honor"), my shoulder-length hair felt heavy. Hot. The Vietnam War was not over but I felt in need of a change. I walked into a barbershop on University Avenue.

"Yes?" the nearest barber asked. He was clearly surprised to have a long-hair in his shop.

"I'd like a haircut," I answered.

"I'd say," said another, older barber with no small sarcasm. He gestured to an open chair.

I settled in, the barber swirled the blue chair cloth down over me, taped it around my neck, then began to whack away.

"But save my hair," I said suddenly; it tumbled to the floor in thick brown leaves.

"Say what?" the barber asked; he paused with his scissors.

"I want to save my hair," I said. "When you're done cutting, I want it swept up and bagged." I had developed an edge of my own; the big university, the city streets were inside me now. I knew what I wanted and was not afraid to say so.

"Okay, kid," he said with a shake of his head and continued the shearing.

That haircut was one of the worst I've ever had, but I did not much care about how I looked then. I was full of simmering anger and restlessness. On the way home from the barbershop I took my grocery bag of curly brown hair to the post office, taped the bag shut, addressed it to my father, and mailed it. In our relationship, it is the act I most regret. He did not deserve that.

My father had always taken on extra jobs to help pay for my sister Judy and me at college. His work as county weed inspector entailed miles of walking—just what his legs did not need—to respond to calls about noxious weeds, including hoary alyssum, spotted knapweed, and wild mustard. Farmers were responsible for weed control in their fields, and most were good about it; however, my father's job was to assist those who "needed help," that is, were remiss. He went to the farm, measured the outbreak (which might be several acres), and arranged for spraying and, if necessary, financial assistance from the county.

I often helped him "run chain" with a measuring device that I always admired: a hand-held, open-faced wheel wound full with a thin, silvery metal tape. The narrow steel ribbon was threaded through the eyelets of a gaggle of small metal rods. As my father limped across a field the tape unwound behind; he paused intermittently to poke a rod into the ground, then moved on, the tape stretching across the field like a miniature, glinting power line. When he had recorded the distance, measured in real rods, each of which is sixteen feet, he cranked the handle and drew up the tape back onto the wheel. The farthest rod loosened first from

the earth and as the glinting tape drew it toward the next
and the next the growing cluster came clanking across the
field trailing dust and loosening bull thistle silk in the summer air. Finally drawn all together at the reel, the little rods
tinkled against each other like wind chimes.

Sometimes, in long fields, I ran the tape for him, and
during those summers I learned my weeds: yellow rocket,
white cockle, lamb's quarter, rough pigweed, blue vervain,
wild buckwheat, witchgrass. I have his weed seed identifica-
tion chart. It is a cardboard square with fifty-six holes, like a
checkers-type game board, each filled with seeds and sealed
over with a plastic sheet. Seeds such as rough cinquefoil are
as tiny as grains of sand. Leafy spurge is the size of coarse
salt. Jimson weed and field bindweed are as big and dark as
peppercorns. When I hold the chart and shake it now, the
seeds, in their clear-eyed pockets, rattle like fine castanets.

Chapter Six

A railroad cleaved through our family of farms. It separated Gerry's place from mine, but the crossing, with its slivered planks and tire-burnished bolts, was a meeting spot, and the railroad bed a boy's highway. Almost daily we walked it west a mile to our grandfather's place and sometimes beyond, to the edge of town two more miles away. East took us two miles to Dorset, a town of thirty or so with a lumberyard, bait shop, and café. Beyond Dorset was uncharted territory—the edge of the earth—so we settled for a candy bar or an ice cream cone at the café in Dorset, then turned back.

Along the way we made forays into the fields to check our gopher traps just in case (we had already checked them once) but always returned to the railroad bed, where we looked for shiny red agates in the dull gravel around the ties, the heavy wooden beams that held up the iron rails. The ties wafted up a sweet, baked, chemical smell of creosote, and each tie carried a round-faced, gray metal tack on its butt end with a number stamped on it: the date of installation. If

Gerry or I spotted one that was particularly old (I remember seeing a 1937), we called out the year. The iron rails themselves, polished on top by train car wheels and anchored to the ties by heavy brackets and railroad spikes, shimmered away before us and behind. A quarter-mile in either direction the rails narrowed to a meeting point—a mirage, of course—but one that left us, no matter how far we had walked, exactly in the middle of our day's travels.

My father had wanted to be a railroad engineer. This was easy to imagine—on the order of a boy wanting to be a fireman: what was not to like about the daily train and its whistle? An orange, Great Northern diesel locomotive pulled a half-dozen rust-colored boxcars followed by several open-faced pulp cars ricked high with aspen or spruce logs. The latter threw out a wash of fresh, piney scent as the cars thundered past, and the rails—impossibly rigid when Gerry and I walked them—undulated beneath the iron wheels. The train always ended with a caboose, a stubby, boxy, green-colored car with one guy lounging inside. He usually smoked a cigarette and had a window open and one elbow hanging out as he rode along facing backward, the rails and land always receding behind. Men in cabooses sometimes waved to small boys. "That's what I want to do when I grow up!" Gerry remarked more than once.

My father wanted to run the locomotive—to head "out West" as we called it then and now, and through the mountains. My mother often said it would have been a good thing for him to get away from his family: to be on his own. And he might have tried for an engineer's job but for his polio. Attitudes toward the handicapped were far narrower in the 1940s and 1950s, but prejudice was not the issue. My father always believed he could have passed the tests, physical and otherwise, but he felt that if he sat down he would never get up. That he had to be upright on a regular basis—keep his legs moving or they would fail him.

The corridor of the railroad tracks also carried telegraph and telephone lines. Telegraph poles were older, weathered, with drooping lines; telephone poles were taller and newer, their thinner wires more tautly strung—the wind through them hummed a higher note. Both kinds of poles had wooden cross arms and glass insulators that supported the wires. The blue and the clear glass cones (blue ones were older), about the size of a coffee mug, kept the wires removed from the wooden support arms and preserved the current—the millions of tiny clicks and voices that I imagined I heard murmuring in the wires. The insulators glowed blue and glassy when sunlight caught them and were natural targets for boys with slingshots and .22 rifles; however, there was big trouble in that, and we nearly always gave the glass fixtures a pass.

The telegraph lines were the first to fall silent, and my father was quick to collect, with permission from the railroad authorities, large spools of the wire, which was useful in many ways on the farm. Baling wire was darker, thinner, and more brittle—hard to work with; telegraph wire was thicker, softer, easy to snip yet impossible to break. It was particularly good for fences, for temporary repairs on hay wagons, and as anchor wires on my father's coyote and fox traps.

"We need to get as much of it as we can," my father said one Saturday morning when we already had gleaned most of a pickup load of telegraph wire—a giant nest of hand-rolled spools. "Enough so we never run out."

I was a teenager then, not happy with this particular Saturday project, and I made some mildly sarcastic comment.

"We'll use it all," my father said. "You'll see."

When I was in junior high school, my father and I were still close in our own mute way. In October, he often picked me up after school to go grouse hunting. He had a lunch packed, or else we stopped up in town at a diner attached to the barbershop and had a sweet roll with coffee for him and a grape or orange "pop" for me. After that, we headed to the woods.

For partridge, my father was a road hunter. The middle of the week was a good time to drive slowly down the logging trails on county and state land, looking for ruffed grouse that fed on the clover or perched on a roadside log to take the sun, males with their mottled, rusty-brown tail feathers erect in a perfect fan in case a lady grouse should happen by. We idled along in silence, the truck in low gear, for miles. He watched his side, I mine. We never shot partridge from inside the vehicle but were not averse to killing a grouse sitting in the middle of the trail. Their dun-colored meat, nearly all breast, was a wild game favorite, on the order of pheasant but with a slight taste of the woods. Of leaves. When I was young, partridge meat tasted like freshly split aspen wood smelled, and later, when I was older and had traveled, it tasted like a rare, dry white wine. My mother pan-fried partridge in buttery white gravy swimming with bits of crust and giblets, and so on road hunts my father and I made certain to have a bird or two in hand before we took our chances with wing shots in the bush.

Often a trail-side grouse scuttled into the brush at the sight of the pickup (sometimes we heard dry leaves rustle and only then pinpointed the bird), at which I jumped out and went after him. I used a .410 shotgun, a bolt-action "single barrel," meaning it held only a single shell. It was the perfect starter gun for a young hunter, lightweight and easy to swing but without heavy recoil. However, in the long seconds it took to step out of the truck, uncase the gun, and load it, the bird got a considerable head start. Once in the thick undergrowth, a grouse freezes in place. Its mottled brown and white and gray feathers merge with leaves and twigs as if painted with the same palette, the same brush. The bird becomes landscape. A hunter's only chance is to make the partridge fly.

In baseball a batter has a half-second or less to pull the trigger on a good fastball; with grouse hunting the timing is about the same. On a baseball field the rules are clear: the pitcher is always on the mound sixty feet away. In the woods a grouse might be to the left or right, or underfoot, or behind you—or might launch itself from a tree branch above you. The latter shot is almost impossible, probably like trying to hit a major league slider breaking down and away. On the other hand, pitchers make mistakes and groove a fastball, and grouse occasionally flush straight ahead down the open tunnel of the brush-lined trail.

After a kill, we always examined the bird. My father opened the feathered breast skin with a quick, tearing motion, and with his little jackknife slit open the crop in order to see its contents. The milky little globe bulged with aspen or tag alder buds, along with bright green clover leaves and small, red and white Viburnum berries. Many hunters yank back the skin, cut away the breast, then toss the feathery, skinny-legged carcass into the woods. We always took our grouse home whole and skinned it fully in order not to waste a bite of meat. The firm, white-flesh breast often had a wispy dark tendril or two of feather protruding from it—where the fine shot had penetrated—and these we excised with a fillet knife (the goal was to avoid encountering a lead shot between the teeth during supper and a possible trip to the dentist). But finding a shot in a forkful was not uncommon, either, and anyone who ate wild fowl knew enough to chew carefully—and to spit a little pellet into one's napkin without making a fuss about it. In our family, we considered finding a lead shot a small kind of luck.

On the same September trip as the grouse-hunting mishap in Montana, Rose and I visited some Idaho backcountry. I had a shirttail relative there, a hermit by the name of Hans. He was from my uncle Jim's wife's side of the family tree—a far branch who lived deep in the Salmon River country. Since I would be in the neighborhood, I promised Uncle Jim that I would stop and see "Old Hans" and report on his health (he was death on doctors).

After forty miles of gravel road along the Salmon River beside increasingly close walls of soaring rock, we found his little cabin. Hans was in good repair, a crusty, eccentric old guy who believed in astrology and other signs and portents and who wore high rubber boots (without socks) 24/7 against the threat of rattlesnakes. On the continuum of "normal," Hans would have found a friend in my great-uncle Emil Swenson. Chickens came and went through the open door of Hans's cabin—but were wise enough to stay just out of reach. In preparation for supper that night he blasted one out of a tree with a shotgun; after a less than thorough plucking and dressing, he boiled the chicken in a pot on his gas stove, the grates of which were bearded with stalactites of old grease. Rose and I ate lightly. Rather than sleep in the cabin, we pitched our tent in his yard and slept beside the steady churning of the Salmon River, below granite cliffsides that soared straight upward to the moon.

In the morning I was eager to go hunting. I had along my trusty twelve-gauge Remington pump, and Rose and I headed up a steep but grassy trail. Not far along we encountered a diamondback rattlesnake. It was coiled and buzzing—not ready to let us pass—and I quickly shot it. I suppose I could have found a stick and pitched the rattler over the bank, but I was quick on the trigger then. A bit farther on, a partridge flushed from a thick stand of alders. I swung and fired—the bird dropped. Rose held my shotgun as I scrambled down the steep bank and into the saplings to retrieve the bird. I brought back the grouse—held up its warm, downy body to show her.

"That's amazing," she said. "You shot its head off."

I did not tell her that I had never made such a good shot in my life and have not since.

The railroad tracks that ran past the farm figured strongly in our family hunting life. They offered an easy walk for partridge, which liked the sunny edges of brush on the north side, but the railway figured more strategically in deer hunting. Deep in the woods of my grandfather's farm was The Cut. This was a wide, glacier-gouged swale that ran north-south through eighty acres of brush and timberland, the side hills of which were too steep to clear and farm—and which also presented a challenge to the railroad builders. But nothing stopped the march of railroad iron, and The Cut—about a hundred yards wide and close to fifty feet deep—had been filled entirely by the labor of men and horses. This created a high-banked bed for the railroad tracks (so high that it was scary to walk across when I was very young), but its damming effect also created natural game corridors. On both ends was a heavily used deer crossing.

My father's deer stand was positioned at the west side
of The Cut, at the north edge of the woods on the side hill
by a Rural Electric Association pole. Every fall we delivered
a fresh bale of straw to the base of the pole. It was important to get the bright yellow, sharp-smelling straw bale (the
twine, chemically treated against nibbling rodents, was more
pungent than the straw) in position well before deer season
in order to let the wind and sun dissipate its color and scent.
For the hunt, my father parked his pickup a few yards away,
out of sight in the brush, and with a walking stick navigated
the rough ground to his straw bale seat—which also held
in the heat of his legs. On those gray November days, with
a blanket over his lap and with some dried weeds or light
brush drawn up around his boots, he was nearly indistin-
guishable from the REA pole.

His view commanded east across The Cut as well as
the main deer trail at the west end—only thirty yards to the
side and slightly below. By the 1970s, even his brothers ac-
knowledged that my father could no longer "drive" (that is,
walk), and so this prime spot became his. Gerry and I were
resigned to being drivers, trampers, and brush beaters until
our fathers died—the epiphany of which (I was in my twen-
ties at the time) was a kind of blue sky moment. I stopped
resenting the hard slogs through the brush and began to
take great pride in tracking a deer—real hunting, as I saw
it—and trying to push one out to my father's gun.

On one of those colorless November days, the drivers
gathered on the gravel road a half-mile south of the railroad
tracks. We spread out in an irregular picket, about a hundred
feet apart, and waited long minutes in silence to make sure
the standers were in place. A thin, needling snow fell; a light

breeze quartered to the southeast. Usually it was the oldest driver who gave a hand signal to move into the woods, but I had slowly come, over the years, to gather some authority. I was a good shot, a jump shooter who could knock down a deer when it leaped from its bed, one who seldom fouled up (there are endless ways to miss a deer). On this day, the Weaver cousins and a couple of their friends, locals who knew the drill, looked to me for direction. In hunting, it nearly always pays to wait just a bit longer; I gestured accordingly. Two of the youngest cousins, knowing they had the brushiest, lowest cover to fight through, stamped their feet impatiently. They just wanted to get this over with.

Hunting is largely about the weather and time. There are confluences of temperature, light, and wind when the odds are stacked against the hunter. An overly warm or a bitterly cold day, too much sun or too little, dry leaves that make for loud woods, swirling and inconsistent wind—any of several combinations make the chance of shooting a deer like winning the lottery: while it conceivably could happen, it is not likely. At other times, like that day, conditions favor the hunter. Low barometric pressure. Damp, gray, chilly skies. Light snow drifting straight down, muffling sound and scouring the air. Human scent does not travel well; like wood smoke falling down the sides of a cabin on a still day, it pools at ground level, stays close to the body. Underfoot, the oak leaves were limp and soundless. There was an incipience: something was going to happen.

I finally signaled our line forward, and we entered the woods. With rifle at the ready, I walked a minute.

Stopped.

Watched ahead and to all sides.

Faint thrashing sounds came from the younger cousins fighting through the brush. I glanced behind, then moved forward again.

About a hundred yards into the woods, two deer—small ones—bounced up and bounded forward out of sight. Marchers halted; we passed a silent wave up and down the line. The deer were headed in the right direction, and we pressed on.

Halfway to the railroad tracks the timber grew taller, and in the swale the brush thickened. On a steep, oak-covered side hill, I spotted a bare oval of brown oak leaves—a deer's bed. From the size of it, a buck had lain here. I knelt and put my bare palm on the leaves. They were not warm, but not cool, either. It was a perfect spot to lie and watch: the buck could see in all directions, take the breeze into his snout—plus, he had two quick escape routes, one high, one low.

I paused over his tracks, big, wedge-like triangles. They were pointed in the right direction, but I held back. To the sides, I saw glimpses of orange as the other drivers struggled through the tangled brush. When I caught Gerry's attention, I pointed to the ground—to the deer bed—then to the sides and forward. Hand signals, catcher to pitcher. Our own language. He waved back and moved forward.

I eased sideways to the nearby brush fall and hunkered down by it to break my silhouette. The snow continued to fall and at a quickened pace, enough that I had to blink and blink to see well. I was glad to have an open sight—"iron sights"—on my .30–06 rifle; a telescopic sight would have been useless in the snow.

A few minutes later two shots barked farther east—not my father's gun—and then a shout somewhere along the line, the pop of a smaller gun—one of the younger cousins. Someone called, "I hit him!" The woods were silent again.

Whenever there is action on the drive, the spell is broken. The forward line breaks; the drivers, especially the younger hunters, forget their task in order to hurry among the trees toward whoever fired the shots. Curiosity. Relief, perhaps, that their work is over.

I waited. Five minutes. Longer. I took off the glove from my shooting hand so that I could feel the bare trigger iron of my rifle; I got ready.

The buck and I saw each other at the same time. He was sneaking back through the broken picket line, head low, weaving his antlers through the underbrush; I saw him as he lifted his head to look at me. I threw up my rifle, but he whirled like a heavy brown trout in a swift current and was gone.

Sometimes hunting means running. I jumped up and raced like a crazy man, flailing through brush in order to cut off the buck's passage. Sweitzer Lake lay just over the side hill, and I managed to reach the slope from where I could see all the way down to the ice—and have a clear shot should the buck turn fully south. He didn't show.

After I caught my breath, I worked my way east, then west, east then west in widening swings until I picked up his trail—scuffed oak leaves across the snow. The trail was obvious at first—a running track—then less so as he slowed and began to sneak.

Occasionally his tracks turned sideways: he had stopped to look over his shoulder. Lift his nose and take in the air. A deer will "snort," or whistle, when surprised; however, the sound is not an exhalation but a sucking in of air—a quick noseful to parse out a scent that should not be in the woods. A spooked deer will always remain silent.

As we moved forward, me on his tracks, him out of sight but not far ahead, it was clear that he wanted to turn back. Each time I correctly guessed his intent and direction—and pushed him forward again. Suddenly ahead, over at the east field, a pickup motor started, then came voices of my cousins and the thud of the pickup's door. They were clear of the woods, but I knew my father would remain on his stand until I came out to him.

Barely fifty yards from The Cut—I could see patches of its wide, blank face beyond the aspens and oaks—I lost the buck's trail. It disappeared. I backtracked but found nothing. I let out a long breath, stood up straight, and slung my rifle over my shoulder. It had been a good hunt, a good try. It was enough.

My father's rifle report rocked the woods—a single shot—and I hurried forward even as the echo fell away into the trees.

At the southwest edge of The Cut lay the buck, a long and beautiful animal, its brown sides heaving, rear legs thrashing but slowing even as I approached. I held my rifle at the ready—my father once broke a rifle stock in defense against a lunging, injured deer—but this one was dead. A single shot to the neck. Clean kill.

I stepped into the open where my father could see me and pumped an arm. He waved back. He stood up only now, his shoulders and cap shrouded with snow. Using his walking stick, it took him a few minutes to make his way down to the trail. I took the buck by his antlers and dragged him forward. His smooth-haired sides slid easily on the snow and flopped twice across the iron rails. It was not a heavy animal, but it had tall, pale, elegant antlers—a beautiful ten-pointer.

"One shot," my father said as we met.

I could only smile.

"I saw him once, but he turned back. I figured you were on him," he added. He kept his voice down—it was just something we did when in the woods.

"I was," I said, still out of breath, steaming with heat. I took off my jacket and rolled up my sleeves and got out my knife.

"He's not as big as I thought," my father observed.

"But a beautiful rack," I said. I hoisted the animal part-way up the bank so the blood would run downhill and then began to field-dress him. It was an unspoken ritual between us; whoever killed the deer got a pass on the gutting. Got time to come down from the kill.

I started at the buck's business end, cutting carefully around his cock and balls, making sure not to nick the bladder or the anal tube that led inward to the stomach; then, knife edge up and two fingers below it in a V-shaped guide, I made the long incision forward up the belly to the cleft of the rib cage. Beneath me the snow was a widening crimson rug. Turning my face away from the fatty, hot breath of the chest cavity, I rolled out the gut sack while my father hoisted the deer by his antlers still higher in order to drain the last of the blood. My final task was to remove the heart and lungs. I reached upward, elbow-deep into the chest cavity; it is an act done best by feel, and I closed my eyes to better follow the location of my knife—and to make sure I did not cut off a finger.

We were not heart-eaters, but I saved the warm, purple fruit nonetheless; someone would be happy to take it home, slice it thin, and fry it in butter to crispy, brown rosettes. When I finished, the blood from the chest cavity had firmed to clots of dark gelatin. I stood up and washed my hands with snow as my father continued to admire the antlers.

"You should have him mounted," I said.

"It's awful expensive," he said.

I was silent. The wet snow on my wrists and forearms melted to a watery pink, and he handed me a paper towel, which we always carried in our pockets for this occasion.

But then he said, "Maybe I will get him mounted. They don't get much prettier than this one."

The rest of our party approached. Someone brought around the pickup. Cousins and uncles gathered near the buck, and then they loaded him for us, which was another of those unspoken rituals among our family: whoever killed the deer did not have to lift or carry. We lingered in the bluing snow, Uncle Emery with his old .35 Remington, wearing his ancient, red wool jacket; Uncle Jim, taller, with his newer .308 rifle (the brothers never agreed upon guns); my cousins with various lesser rifles and a shotgun here and there; neighbor Bill Williams in tattered Canadian wool pants and his short-barreled, well-worn, slide-action .30–06 slung over his shoulder. We went over the story of the drive. Of who saw what. Of who had gone where. We joshed with a cousin or uncle who had missed a shot or gotten turned around in the deep woods. Our hunting coats absorbed the snowflakes that landed on our shoulders and caps in the fine, red wool hair, then melted and disappeared. Our breath smoked in the chilly air, and in the rear of the pickup the dead buck sent up wisps of steam. None of us were in a hurry to leave, but soon enough the air turned colder and it was time to call it a day.

In this winter gloaming my father and I drove home. We followed the bumpy service trail that ran alongside the railroad tracks and the old telephone lines. At the county road crossing, he braked; from habit, he looked both ways down the tracks. I did, too, but we need not have. By that year, the trains had stopping running altogether.

Chapter Seven

At the university I fell increasingly under the spell of great books, art, and ideas. This life of the mind carried me increasingly afield from hunting and the land—as did another event: I fell in love with a city girl.

I met her in Shakespeare class at the University of Minnesota in the winter of 1971 on the third floor of the Mechanical Engineering building (which adjoined the English department's building), in one of those overheated classrooms with rococo, hissing radiators and frosted-over windows. The bitter cold of January had a constricting effect on war protests, and literature was a great escape from the chaos at street level. By then I was a full-fledged English major with the zeal of a new convert—and carried away by Shakespeare. Under the instruction of Professor Shirley Garner, a poised and attractive woman (like the best teachers, she led from the rear), nearly every line of *King Lear* or *The Tempest* was a closed blossom to be sniffed, a hard candy teased around my tongue until its Elizabethan meter was fully felt. I sat up front. I was eager to hear and be heard. There were a couple of other quick-to-speak young men like me with bushy hair and sweaters that needed washing, and we competed for Dr. Garner's attention; one of us (it might have been me!) once stood atop a classroom table in order to declaim some lines. It was at least halfway into the term before I noticed the beautiful girl in the back of the room.

The Tempest receded as if blown out to sea. In its place were the rainbow cuffs of the girl's bell-bottom jeans, her long legs, and an odd, kind calm that she carried about her. She did not notice me sneaking looks at her. As class continued, she followed Professor Garner's instruction with a detached though sympathetic gaze. Her eyes were a neutral blue. Occasionally a ghost of a smile crossed her face; once, her lips moved. She was a totally unselfconscious woman with long hair, streaked platinum, and the fine features of Grace Kelly (I had not seen many movies and only later would understand that comparison).

I do not remember the rest of *The Tempest* or much else about that term. Over the last few weeks I migrated, seat by seat, toward her desk. I made sure to say hello—casually, in passing—if I saw her before or after class. A couple of times I followed her a block or so and was struck by how she did not look to the side nor behind her. She usually got onto the red, No. 16A bus, which whirred away, leaving me shivering on the snowy sidewalk of University Avenue as the tide of forty thousand students flowed and eddied around me. I tried to divine her life; I knew that it was not centered upon the Tragedies and the Comedies.

I did not gather up courage to make a move until nearly the last day of class. I managed to sit at the desk directly ahead of her and to make some small talk before class and get her phone number. I waited a tasteful couple of days before calling but in the end was overeager.

"HithisisWillfromShakespeare," I said in a rush.

There was a long pause. "Right," she said. "Who is this really?"

Her life was focused upon a couple of part-time jobs and a small, off-campus apartment on Ashland Avenue that she shared with two other girls of similarly slender means. The three women ate lots of tuna, which meant that I had a high card to play.

The farm provided me an endless supply of food—a pipeline of beef, venison, frozen chickens, partridge, walleyed pike, as well as all manner of homemade jams, jellies, and pickles, and wild rice. I went home about once a month; I always came back to my university apartment with a suitcase heavy with food.

By then I had also come to acquire the affectations of a Literary Man, including a World War II–era, ankle-length gabardine trench coat with lambswool collar. The coat was more heavy than warm, but with its belt cinched around my waist and collar up around my ears I was mostly protected from the bitter, northwest wind that swirled down the Mississippi River channel and across the Washington Avenue Bridge, which linked the east and west banks of the campus. My trench coat, an army-surplus bomber hat, and pipe. The pipe was as much reading aid as literary prop—one bowl of pungent, dark tobacco and I could read Dostoevsky until dawn—but my largest presumption centered upon food: because I had lots of it, I came to think that I was a good cook. A gourmet, even.

I was without a girlfriend when I met Rose, in part because of an incident in the kitchen with a previous girl. I was cooking steaks, and Carla volunteered to help make the salad, a process which I micromanaged and ultimately took over but not before admonishing her for cutting the lettuce with a knife instead of tearing it by hand. It was the beginning of the end with Carla. Rose was not so delicate and suffered my pretensions in return for a serious steak. It was she, however, who showed me that salads were more than iceberg lettuce and grated carrots with French dressing slathered on top and that a good T-bone steak need not be cooked until it was gray in the middle—nor did it require gravy.

I eventually met her parents, Vincent and Rosalie, whose St. Paul, Catholic life felt much like small-town living but with nicer tableware. Her family used cloth napkins most days and Waterford crystal on Sundays. At first they treated me cheerfully, easily, with few questions asked; I was just a nice boy from college. However, when I began picking up their daughter every day from work and regularly cooking meat for her at my apartment, their manner became measured, if not downright concerned. As a student of the liberal arts I was, as Dickens wrote, a man of "little capital and few prospects." This is not to say that her family was well-off or focused on money; Rose's mother did not work or even drive, and their family blessings were more in children (five), good genes, and handsome features than in property or portfolios. But in the back of her parents' mind had to have been the inescapable fact: their beautiful daughter was perfectly capable of marrying a doctor or lawyer, as opposed to a bushy-haired English major from the north woods.

I had my own worries. I wanted to bring her home to the farm—show her *my* real life—but I worried that I might break whatever spell I had cast. Not long into our dating life she confessed that, by my manner in class, she thought I was from the East Coast.

I laughed.

"What's so funny?" she asked evenly.

I fumbled with my reply—by then she knew I was from a farm—but I was not ready to share the real details of farm life. My old-world dairy barn with its wooden stanchions. The rank smell of calf pens. The dark winter mountain of manure. The frozen deer blood that lingered all winter on the tailgate of my father's pickup. The cold garage hung with frozen fox and coyotes. The carcasses of skinned beaver and mink and raccoons that we tossed into the hayloft as winter food for the barn cats; the clattering, dried skeletons I removed in spring with a pitchfork. The sick cow that had to be dragged, bellowing, from the barn by rope and tractor, then shot. Hunting and blood trails and butchering and farm accidents—all of this I held back from her.

But in March, at the beginning of spring break, we headed north to meet my parents. The four-hour drive felt very long. I had forgotten how many times the highway crossed the Mississippi River and how much the road narrowed and the trees closed in as we pushed on. We arrived at the farm in falling dark. It looked small beneath the high, late-winter snowbanks. Narrow, white house. Wooden granary. Sagging pig house, no longer used. Tall hay shed still a third full (a good sign) of dusky green alfalfa bales. The looming, blank face of the dairy barn. Its windows were unlit and gray, which meant milking was over; my parents and Carl, the hired man, were waiting supper. They usually ate at five-thirty; it was already seven.

Greetings went well. I had prepared Rose for everything, I thought, including Carl, who was washed up nicely

and did not smell of the barn. We were barely into our supper—a major meal of thoroughly cooked roast beef, gravy,
and all the trimmings—when a yowling came from outside.
Snow muffled the sound, which came from the windbreak
close by the north side of the house, and at first we ignored
it. But as supper went on, the yowling grew in frequency and
volume. "Carl," my father finally said, and jerked his head
toward the door.

Carl lurched up from the table and disappeared. We
went on with dinner, and soon Carl came back. "Old tomcat!" he said in his guttural, froggy voice. "A bad, wild one."

"Bud," my father said, nodding discreetly at me this
time.

"Excuse me," I said cheerfully to Rose. "I'll be right
back."

On the porch (out of sight from the kitchen table) I
found the single-shot twelve gauge in the broom closet—
every farmer had an old shotgun handy for emergencies—
dug around for a shell, and went outside. The ancient tomcat
was ten feet or so up in a spruce tree, growling and screech-
ing in pain—bowel obstructed, distempered, something dire.
His ears were frozen off to nubs, and his orange fur was
patchy with mange—an old tom had come near the house
to commit suicide by farmer. My shotgun charge blew him
from the limb, and he tumbled, dead, into the deep snow.
I returned to the porch, put away the gun, washed my hands
in the cold sink, then came into the kitchen and took my
place again at the table. Conversation continued. No one
mentioned the shotgun blast. Dinner went on smoothly, ending with apple pie and ice cream. Afterward, alone with Rose,
I murmured, "Sorry about the cat thing."

"It's okay—no problem!" she replied a bit too quickly.

That evening I was surprised to find that my mother had made sleeping arrangements for Rose and me, together, in my old bedroom. As we cozied under heavy quilts under the steep eaves, I saw my little room through her eyes: the frosted-over window, the shadowed mementos of sports and hunting, the demolition derby trophy, the frilly garter from my senior prom that dangled from a set of whitetail antlers, the closet with no door, only a curtain on a thin rod. In fact, my bedroom had no door, only a heavier rod and drape-type curtain. It was all so small, poor, and rural. But she seemed to channel my thoughts and pulled me tighter to her.

The next morning we toured the farm. The snow was still too deep for walking much beyond the plowed yard. We had a peek inside the dairy barn; she was surprised at its warmth as we walked along the front, manger side of the rows of Holstein dairy cows. Then we took a look in the tall, wooden granary and afterward climbed up the bales in the hay shed, where we got a good view of the lay of the land—its fields and pines—to the west. I did not show her behind the barn where Carl pitched the winter's manure from the gutter, or take her into the cold garage where the rafters were hung with my father's winter trapping: fox, coyotes, beavers, mink, raccoons, the odd otter, some of them skinned and some still in the carcass. It was her first trip to the farm, and I wanted to go lightly on dead animals.

Late that morning we drove the short mile to Sweitzer Lake, where I chipped out a half gunnysack's worth of ice, then with the flat side of an axe smashed it into finer slivers. At home, my mother had prepared the batter for homemade ice cream, using real cream skimmed from raw milk—and not just any milk. My father, like many dairy farmers, kept some "color" in his herd—a few yellow Guernsey cows mixed in with the black-and-white Holsteins to keep up the butterfat. If the fat content of Holstein milk was about 3.5 percent, Guernsey milk was nearly twice that much—from its richness it had a slightly yellow cast—and its cream was thick enough to float a spoon.

We took turns cranking the old wooden cylinder, adding rock salt to the ice chips, feeling the crank turn with increasing difficulty.

Once I stumbled mid-crank and had to reverse directions and start again. "It's not like we do this every day!" I said to Rose, partly to make a joke but partly, I realized, to clarify that we actually bought our ice cream at stores.

"Only on special occasions," my mother said, smiling. She nudged me aside to take a turn. Afterward, we ate large bowls of the pale, vanilla-scented ice cream that was rich enough to make me sweat and which brought color to Rose's cheeks as well.

Afterward, as we packed to leave, my mother took me aside and said, "I'm so pleased that you came home. And that Rose—for a Catholic, she's such a nice girl!"

I could only laugh and say, "I know what you mean."

The final act of packing was, of course, to open the big, chest-type freezer in the porch and load up on meat. Rose's eyes widened at the largesse of white freezer paper packages, each neatly labeled "Steak" or "Chops" or "Beef Roast" or "two mallards" or "four walleye." Each was dated. Some packages of beef carried the name of the butchered steer (Carl usually called them "Billy," which then required further distinctions such as "Little Billy" and "Big Billy" and "Kicker Billy"). When rummaging through the freezer I tried not to be greedy, but my mother kept pressing more packages of meat upon us. She also made us a lunch "for the long ride home."

Rose slept much of the way back to the city—it had been a successful but not necessarily an easy weekend. Or maybe it was the rich ice cream that made her doze against me. Whatever the reason, I drove as carefully as I ever had in my life so as not to awaken her and was as happy as I had ever been. I could feel my life of the farm and woods receding behind me; I knew it would never come back all the way, but I did not care. She woke by the time we reached the northern suburbs—it was dusk—and then snuggled against me as we pressed onward toward the brightening city lights.

Chapter Eight

My high school life in Park Rapids, Minnesota, a farm town of 2800, was a closed orbit of local girls, sports, cars, and hunting—a Springsteen song without the tragedy. I kept a shotgun in the back seat of my '57 Chevy and a scatter of shells in the glove box (not recommended today). After school let out, my best friend, Jeff, and I headed to the woods. We both played basketball but not football, and while I ran on the cross-country team to be in shape for winter hoops, there was still plenty of time to hunt ducks and partridge. The deer season was no problem, either; school let out for several days, and no clear-thinking person would schedule any serious event during the first two weeks of November.

Jeff was a townie. I'm not sure how we met—probably on the basketball floor—but he was a blond-haired, friendly kid who liked outdoors stuff but whose parents were golf and country club–type people. His father was a math teacher, his mother a dental hygienist, and they lived in a tidy, "suburban" (for our town), 1950s-style rambler on North Main Street. The Anderson house had a picture window, a sunburst

clock, a console stereo, and actual carpet (as opposed to li-
noleum) on the living room floor. Things were always neat
and orderly at Jeff's house, which is why, I think, he liked to
come to the farm. There we could shoot guns. Drive tractors.
Work on cars. Make a bonfire. Blow things up with cherry
bombs. My parents liked Jeff a good deal, and he became
a brother to me and a regular at the supper table; he also
learned a lot about hunting from my father.

Before Jeff and I got our driver's licenses, my father took
us partridge and duck hunting a couple of times a week in October. One of the first lessons learned was about obeying the
law. Shotguns (the repeating type as opposed to the double-
barrel) have a magazine-type tube that can hold up to five
shells. To give ducks and geese a break, Minnesota law (as
well as the law in most other states) requires that hunters
install a plug—a short piece of wooden dowel rod—in the
magazine to reduce the shell count to three. Plugs were easy to
remove, however. One October afternoon Jeff and I executed
a long sneak on a narrow slough—which we found loaded
with ducks. My father was a quarter-mile away, back at the
truck, and there were occasional gun reports from other hunters in the area. As we lay hunkered in the cattails, one of us
(it was probably me) whispered, "Let's take out our plugs!"

"He'll hear us," Jeff said.

"Not if we shoot at exactly the same time," I answered.

Jeff seemed dubious but went along with the scheme.
We unscrewed the magazine caps, shook out the wooden
plugs, then loaded in the extra shells. After crawling within
range—and upon a count of three—we jumped up and
blazed away. Several ducks fell, and the Chesapeake splashed
into the pond to retrieve them. While the dog worked, we
quickly restored our plugs. When all the ducks were in hand,

we headed back to the truck—where my father was waiting, hands on hips.

"You boys case up those guns right now! We're going home."

"What? Why?" I protested.

"You know why," he said.

Jeff got a hangdog, guilty look.

"Why?" I persisted.

"I heard you boys shoot," my father said. "I can count."

Once, soon after Jeff and I were old enough to drive, I almost killed him. We were hunting crows, and our bright idea was for Jeff to perch on the hood of my father's Chevy pickup, holding a shotgun at the ready, while I drove fast down a gravel road toward a grove of oak trees loaded with crows. Neither of us had thought to factor in the braking-of-the-truck part. As we neared the grove I slowed as best I could—we knew better than to shoot at anything from a moving vehicle—but Jeff slid off the hood like a hockey puck on fresh ice. Loaded shotgun clutched in both hands, he tumbled into the ditch. The crows cawed wildly and flapped away. Jeff lay there. I was sure he was dead; on the other hand, his shotgun had not gone off when he hit the ground (the only good news of the moment). I skidded the truck's tires to a full stop and jumped out. He had roused himself by then and staggered upright.

"Jesus! Are you okay?!" I asked.

"Yeah. But we'd better not tell your dad," he said groggily.

While I knew all the farm country trails and sloughs, Jeff had his own eagle eye and sometimes brought news of a big buck on the golf course or late-season northern mallards and snow geese landing on Big Sand Lake. This was "the rich man's lake," as my father called it, a beautiful, round disk of a lake about three miles across and with a hard sand bottom. It had the clearest water in the county and also the biggest homes—most of them second homes owned by wealthy summer residents from Minneapolis or Fargo or Chicago. Big Sand Lake was full of walleye but difficult to access; the lakeshore owners had managed, over time, to restrict the public to a single, cramped boat landing on the south side by the narrow river outlet. Summer nights my father and I sometimes took our little twelve-foot aluminum boat and five-horsepower Evinrude motor to the landing, waiting in line with other locals and their pickups and boat trailers. Once we were launched, my father resolutely steered our little Lund boat at full throttle (about six miles per hour) toward the main body of the lake and the sandbars where the walleye congregated. Big power boats sped past, their wakes rocking us as they pulled tanned, summer girls on water skis. On the shore were cedar docks, diving platforms, and boat lifts for runabouts and Chris-Crafts. Landscaped and irrigated lawns, bright flower beds ringed by fieldstones, the occasional tennis court, flagstone paths that led up to large, log homes, their timbers painted dark brown, or else newer, chalet types with stretching glass fronts and terraces for sunning—the only thing missing from some of the estates was a small, green light on the dock.

"Must be nice," my father often said as we motored past the big houses, but we felt glad just to have access to the lake where, using yellow, buck-tailed jigs tipped with a fresh shiner minnow, we usually took home a stringer of walleye. "You don't need fancy equipment to catch fish," he said. "A yellow jig and a good shiner minnow."

After Labor Day, the Chris-Crafts and the runabouts and the water-skiers were gone. Big Sand, like other lakes, quieted as if someone had turned a giant switch to the "Off" position. Summer homes were locked and shuttered, their pipes having been drained by local caretakers; loons congregated before heading south. Since Big Sand Lake was deeper than most, it was also among the last to freeze over—which made it a perfect place to hunt late-season, migrating mallards and geese.

Jeff was more confident than I was about hunting around the empty lake estates. But he was right: there was no one home. On a scouting trip without guns (a test run), we parked discreetly and walked down a curving, asphalt driveway toward a large, older lake home. Its rear windows were shuttered, but the glass front was not. Inside were leather-and-log furniture and a tall split-rock fireplace; in the kitchen a suspended rack hung with copper pans and orderly rows of wine glasses and champagne glasses. As I was peering inside the house, a noisy gaggle of mallards exploded off the water near the shore.

We flinched and hunkered down.

"See?" Jeff said. "I knew they'd be here."

The ducks had been feeding in the shallow water just out of sight below a short bank—a natural berm pushed up by winter ice tectonics. Most of the homes and cabins along this stretch of the lake had a rounded, beachfront ridge behind which Jeff and I could crawl up on the ducks in broad daylight—which was never a good time for hunting.

"We need to come back when there's some weather," Jeff said, as we watched the mallards fly away, their pale, white wings flashing in the sun. Rain or, even better, light snow always brought ducks and geese down from the sky to feed and wait out a storm before they pushed on, southward.

Over the next week we obsessed on the weather and prayed for winter. Temperatures finally dropped, sealing over ponds and smaller lakes. Ring-neck and other diving ducks clustered in ragged, black rafts on the bigger lakes, and soon Big Sand was the last lake standing. Then came the prediction of snow, a forecast welcomed by all: deer season was past, December had arrived, and people had begun to fret about their septic tanks and their perennials. On one of those dusky, shortened days of early winter, before we had eaten our suppers, Jeff and I packed up our hunting gear and headed after school to the north side of Big Sand Lake. Gray skies, light and wispy snow with more to come later: perfect duck-hunting weather. We parked out of sight of the main road and, with our shotguns in hand, eased along a driveway toward the lake (we avoided walking on the driveway itself in order to leave no tracks in the snow).

We hunkered down along the cold, log side of a big house and, in trying to sneak across the open lawn, spooked a flock of mallards.

"No big deal," Jeff whispered, "there's plenty more."

Which was true. The lake was busy with ducks coming and going—mostly coming—and we crawled quickly to a hiding spot behind a berm. Just as a pair of fat mallards cupped their wings for a landing, Jeff put his hand on my arm.

"Listen!" he said.

I cocked an ear skyward. Geese! The faint, plaintive bark of snow geese, which were uncommon then and harder still to hunt. The geese were somewhere close above; their calls grew louder. The white flock gradually came into sight but well out of shooting range and passed overhead on a downward angle, wings set, their glide path farther out in the lake.

"What do you want to do?" Jeff whispered. Several mallards now paddled within range.

"Let's wait," I said. "There's got to be more geese coming. Some of them were huge!"

"No kidding!" Jeff said, and we hunkered down. I loaded my shotgun with heavy, double-aught buck shells; the goal of hunting is to kill quickly, not cripple or wound.

The snowflakes thickened. The blue gray depth of field closed up like the hoods on our hunting parkas as, against the cold and wet, we drew the nooses ever tighter around our faces. We had to blink and blink to see clearly in the angling whiteness, but finally our patience was rewarded. Sharp, clear yips came from directly overhead—a flock descending from the north. We readied our guns. The geese floated in overhead, lower and lower, ghostly white in the snow, wingspans magnified by the water in our eyes, white on white—enormous geese! We rose to fire, but at the last moment Jeff jerked back his gun and shouted, "No! Don't shoot!"

I did not understand—and anyway it was too late: my gun boomed. One of the big birds came spinning down. Not plummeting—which meant it had been shot dead—but corkscrewing down, one wingtip up, flailing for purchase on the air, the other wing flopping and broken.

"They're swans!" Jeff shouted.

I jerked back my gun as if to retrieve the blast, but a crippled swan now flopped and splashed in the dark water just offshore. Above his long, white neck, his black-masked head swiveled frantically as he looked for his flock—which had flared upward and now was out of sight in the slanting snow and grayness.

I quickly raised my gun again to finish off the bird.

"No—don't!" Jeff called. "Don't shoot again! Somebody might figure out where we are." It was something my father had told us: shoot once, and nobody is quite sure where the shot came from. Shoot twice, and they'll know for certain.

The crippled bird continued to pummel the dark water. I handed my gun to Jeff and scuttled over the bank. Holding up my parka bottom as best I could and hoping that the water would not top my hip boots, I waded forward. My legs were protected by three layers—heavy rubber, jeans, and long underwear—but the water tightened around them like some kind of full-length medical cuff. A heavy, icy constriction. The deeper the water, the greater the weight of its coldness.

As I approached, the big bird tried to flop away but only splashed in circles. I was in nearly hip-deep water by then; the bird's beak and yellow eyes were at my eye level or higher.

"You're gonna drown!" Jeff called. "Come back!"

I managed to grab the swan's neck and plunge the black-masked face underwater—and hold it. The December lake water burned my hands, wrists, and arms; the big wings battered my face and almost knocked me over, but gradually their beating slowed. Stilled. The giant bird went limp.

I dragged it by the neck back to shore. I was not crying, but from the water, the streaming wetness on my face, no one could have told otherwise. I was shuddering from cold, and we quickly headed for the truck. To the side was a patch of brush and near it a pile of leftover limbs cut from a fallen tree. Jeff hid the giant, white bird under the stack of branches, and then we hurriedly drove off. He cranked up the heater in the truck—from the cold I could not have gripped the steering wheel—and drove aimlessly as I warmed up. Intermittently, one of us would begin a sentence.

"Damnit!"

"I should have—"

But anything we said only made things worse. Finally we headed back to the farm, where Jeff got in his own car and drove off to town.

"Jeff couldn't stay for supper?" my mother asked. A plate was set for him.

"Not tonight," I said, avoiding my parents' eyes.

Jeff and I never spoke about the swan again, and no game warden ever came knocking on our doors. Still, it might have been better to have come clean. To have told my father and then taken the big, white swan to town and handed it over to a conservation officer. Taken our punishment. To this day, whenever a late-autumn Minnesota day turns cold, and the gray sky becomes damp and heavy, and snow begins to fall, I think of that swan, how wide and silent its wings—right before I pulled the trigger.

Chapter Nine

I graduated from the University of Minnesota in the spring of 1972 burned out on books. The professor and poet John Berryman, of whom I was a follower, had leapt to his death from the Washington Avenue Bridge that winter. I was sick of literature—did not want to read for a long time—and desperate to reconnect with my real life, whatever that was now.

Still pressed by the draft, I looked high and low in Minneapolis for an alternative service job that would satisfy the requirements of my conscientious objector status. I had no luck. My sister Connie lived in the south San Francisco Bay area, and though I missed Rose terribly, I headed west with the notion that alternative service jobs for COs would be easier to find in San Francisco. There I pounded the pavement, inquiring at hospitals, community organizations, and even large churches—with no success. The selective service kept track of my whereabouts and sent me increasingly ominous mail. Finally, its patience exhausted, the SS (as I had come to call it) ordered me to report to camp in Bishop, California, which was high in the Sierra Nevada, and to bring heavy boots and work gloves. My assignment was to cut brush for two years—the kind of labor I thought I had left back on the farm. From then on, I did not open any more letters from the selective service office. I was prepared to take my punishment (I began to watch my back—to pay attention to suspicious-looking sedans and men in sunglasses), but Richard Nixon, in a surprise move, and bless his black heart, ended the draft in 1973. With it ended my obligation for alternative service. It was a clumsy ending to the question, "What did you do in the Vietnam War, Daddy?" but the Vietnam War had no good endings. Suddenly I was a free man in sunny California.

The muddle with the draft and my status had taken up most of a year after my graduation from college. During that time I had been freeloading off my sister, but now I could look for a real job—any job. My brother-in-law, Don, who was plugged into the burgeoning Silicon Valley electronics industry, told me about a start-up company in Sunnyvale. I showed up the next day in a nondescript industrial park where a few apricot trees had escaped the developer's bulldozer and joined a lobby full of guys looking for work. I applied for a general labor-type job—it seemed like the surest bet; I needed a paycheck and an apartment (Rose, back in St. Paul, was making plans to join me). Not long after I handed in my application, the personnel manager came out of his office and called to the waiting room full of applicants, "Who's the guy from Minnesota?"

I looked around, then held up my hand.

"This way," the man said. I was hired, few questions asked. It was my first experience with what nowadays might be called "place-ism." Minnesotans are well liked in California; the book on us includes words such as "stable" and "dependable." We tend to show up for work on time, if not a day early.

I started as a janitor/handyman—I knew my way around tools—and from there learned the process of making printing circuit boards (a stinky line of electroplating, acid baths, and etching tanks) and then moved into quality control and technical writing. Within six months I was wearing a shirt and tie, had a nice office with a view of a golf course and a secretary out front. I was now a man with some minor capital—at least I could pay rent—and unlimited prospects. Rose arrived, I had an apartment waiting in east San Jose, and we quickly set about making a life together.

She found work at Hewlett-Packard, then a medium-sized electronics company, at its glass-faced headquarters building perched on "The Hill" just across the street from the Stanford campus. Dave Packard and Bill Hewlett still showed up for work. Rose made good money in the international division, and so did I at my printed circuit board company: Silicon Valley was in full swing. On weekends we indulged ourselves in California life—unending sunny days, wine in grocery stores (unheard of in Minnesota), day trips to Napa Valley and the wineries. Fresh artichokes from the fields of Half Moon Bay. Apricots, cherries, and lemons right off the trees. Red snapper straight from the docks at Santa Cruz. Once in a while, at an out-of-the-way restaurant on coastal Highway 1, a meal of abalone. The smell of eucalyptus trees after a rain. Beaches where bathing suits were not necessarily required.

But paradise takes getting used to. After a year or a bit more of the good life, I grew restless. I missed the change of seasons in Minnesota, and hunting in particular. Late nights, while Rose slept, I began to write for the first time about growing up in Minnesota. Farm life. Trapping with my father. Hunting with uncles and cousins. The winter light, the changing of the seasons. I wrote because I was lonesome for the Midwest, and two of these sportsman sketches I turned into short stories.

One piece was about the troop train that came through Minnesota farm country during World War II and stopped in small towns to pick up young men—including my uncle Jim. He once said that it was twenty below zero when he climbed aboard the unheated Pullman car; that the men crowded together to keep warm; that people waited in cars and trucks at country crossings to watch the troop train go by; and that when the train came east past the Weaver farm, all he wanted to do was jump off and go home.

The second story was about deer hunting. When my grandfather Moffet was too old and dim of eyesight to make good use of his deer rifle, his sons (my father and uncles) relieved him of his gun. They gave it to one of the grandsons who could make better use of it. My story focused on my grandfather, who went hunting nonetheless. He sat in the field in his car with the engine idling most of the day, an old shotgun with a single slug at hand even though there was no chance for a deer. A story not about killing but about people. About family.

With vague plans of writing and further study, I sent the stories to Stanford's graduate program in creative writing. The director, Nancy Packer, wrote back to say she liked the stories and that while the Wallace Stegner fellowships had already been awarded, they could offer me a spot in the fiction writing group.

"That was easy," I said to Rose.

In early September, she and I attended the fall semester start-up party for incoming graduate writing students. The event was held just off campus at the tidy, shrub-fronted bungalow of the fiction director. Rose and I arrived on time, which turned out to be early. However, the place gradually filled up with literary types, both faculty members and new grad students, including Raymond Carver, a bearlike guy with squinty eyes. He was greatly pleased to find that Rose and I were from Minnesota—he was from Clatskanie, a sawmill town in Oregon—and more so that I was from a farm.

"We need more real writers here," he said with twinkling eyes.

I came to know Raymond well and to hang out with his merry band, but I struggled in the writing workshop. I was by far the least experienced writer in our group of ten, some of whom came from august literary families and were already publishing their fiction. Feeling the pressure (mostly of my own making), I gradually lost my voice. My way. I forgot the material—the land and woods and hunting—that got me there, but reminders came from surprising directions.

In a class on Yeats, headed by the English poet Donald Davie, we were slogging through the poems and eventually hit Yeats's "Wild Swans at Coole." Some of the PhD-track literature students immediately seized on the symbolism of the swan, from Andromache through Baudelaire's "Le Cygne," and Mallarme's reading of the swan as a figure of literary history. Discussion continued endlessly on the matter of the "virgin" swan and whiteness. I squirmed in my seat. I had a Tourette's-type of need to blurt, "Let me tell you about swans!" But I didn't. But I should have. During those years in California, my connection to the land receded almost to the breaking point.

Intermittently I made attempts to stay in touch with hunting and guns, but they were clumsy and unsuccessful. My sister and her family lived in the Santa Cruz Mountains off winding Highway 17, which ran south from San Jose to the beach at Santa Cruz. Rose and I often drove up for the weekend to hang out and babysit my two nieces and a nephew. Connie and Don were living large—had a big house, hot tub, Porsche, and even their own limousine. Rose and I were happy to watch their kids, Shari, Lisa, and Michael—a very active boy—in return for a break from the noise and traffic of the Bay Area and the cold undercurrents of Stanford.

Those weekends were an opportunity for me to get back to the land. Or at least to a gravel road and some brushy hillsides with eucalyptus trees. The Santa Cruz Mountains had their own country charm. On occasion we could hear the Doobie Brothers (the band itself) practicing from somewhere across the canyon; the hillsides had deer, the occasional mountain lion, plus lots of tasty-looking quail. One Saturday, when my sister's kids were at friends' houses, a covey of quail was feeding in the yard by the swing set. I had been scouting them over several weekends. I knew their patterns.

"We're going to have quail for supper," I announced to Rose.

"You'd better not," she said quickly.

"It'll be easy," I said. "Just one shot."

I resurrected an old shotgun from my brother-in-law's closet (he was a Minnesotan). "A roaster full of quail and a bottle of that Monterey chardonnay for dinner tonight," I said confidently. I loaded a single shell.

I eased along the railing of the wide, redwood deck, then aimed at a plump and oblivious brace of quail; Rose covered her ears and shut her eyes: I fired. The quail—all of them—rocketed away. Rose opened her eyes. Dust drifted where the quail had sat. Dust drifted.

"I missed!" I said.

Something in my voice must have sounded pitiful, because she patted me on the shoulder. "It's okay. There's a frozen pizza in the 'fridge."

On another occasion, my Minnesota college pal Jack, from Montana, came down to the Bay Area for a visit. I was happy to see him—pleased to be around someone who knew guns and the woods—and I also wanted my classmates from the Stanford fiction seminar to meet him and he them. The party at my apartment on Middlefield Drive was going well until he and I got to talking about hunting. From hunting it turned to guns, and at some point I went to the back bedroom and retrieved my shotgun from under the bed. I meant only to show it to Jack. Carrying the gun I walked back to the main party—which quieted as if there had been a power failure. A couple of people slipped out the door; others looked toward it. Several others looked slightly stricken, if not paralyzed.

"What?" Jack asked those who remained. "It's only a shotgun." He laughed a belly laugh and brandished the Remington above his head—a gesture that further reduced congestion in the living room.

Afterward, alone at a bar, he and I had a good laugh about the incident. Rose was not with us; she remained back at the apartment, unamused.

It was during my stint in California that I missed two, or perhaps three, deer seasons. Once I flew back for the November hunt, but the psychic swing—from sun and eucalyptus trees to gray skies and snow—was too wide. I was clumsy.

Off my game. My eyes never fully adjusted to the woods, the forest trails; I felt half blind—as if I were wearing a pair of found glasses. The trip was unsuccessful in nearly every way. The next year when November came around, I called home to get the deer hunting report.

My father was in the barn, but via my mother I learned that my cousin Gerry was using my .30–06 deer rifle.

"What?!" I replied. I was stunned.

"Your father loaned it to him," she explained.

I was speechless.

"I hope that's all right with you?" she added. She had picked up on my surprise.

"Sure," I finally said. "Why not? It's just sitting there."

"That's what your father thought," she said. "He said that Gerry could use it for the time being."

After I rang off, Rose looked at me with concern. "Everything all right in Minnesota?"

"Yes," I said and headed to the spare bedroom where I wrote. Or at least tried to write. Later that night I parsed in my mind the conversation with my mother. "For the time being." Which meant my father still held out hope that I would someday use the rifle again. Me? I was not so sure.

Chapter Ten

We spent four years in California, and in the middle of our time there Rose and I were married in a state park near the Pacific Ocean. None of our parents attended. We did not encourage them, and they did not make the long and expensive trip from Minnesota. The ceremony took place in an A-frame nature interpretive center before a tall stone fireplace; the marriage rites were administered by a Unitarian minister whom we hauled up the hill from the Bay Area in Rose's Volkswagen Beetle.

Wedding guests included Connie and Don (owner of the faulty shotgun and, by now, his own electronics company), plus a large woman who happened to be wandering around the nature center. "Oh, wonderful! A wedding!" she exclaimed and plopped down to watch. A troop of Boy Scouts had been in the building receiving some kind of instruction, but their scoutmaster shooed them outside. I've always thought they could have stayed. It would not have hurt them to see two people so much in love.

When I finished my course work at Stanford, Rose quit her job and we took a belated honeymoon trip to Europe. We visited Rose's younger sister, Mary Jane, who was living in Paris. She had worked in retail clothing at the same St. Paul store as Rose had and during a local modeling event had been "discovered"; she was a lanky, dark-haired beauty—an elongated version of Rose—and was now a high-fashion model. We stayed a few days in her apartment off Saint-Germain, but she was hardly ever home. She was either on assignment or with her boyfriend, Christian, a German photographer, and it was awkward explaining our presence to Mary Jane's roommates, all models, who came and went at all hours.

After a few days in Paris, Rose and I headed on to Dijon to see Terry Davis, a writer friend from my Stanford class whose wife was French. We took a trip in Mariette's little Renault into the Massif Central area, which was hilly and very dry; 1976 was a drought year across Europe and America, and white Charolais cattle clustered along the fences of their brown, stripped pastures. The Charolais were stressed and gaunt, but a French family on its August holiday had stopped for a roadside picnic and asked us to take a photograph of them in front of the panting cows. I had never felt so lonesome for the Midwest.

Rose and I returned to California broke but happy to be back—and ready to get serious about life. We returned to the Midwest, and, after a short stop in St. Paul, I went all the way home. My father was thinking about retiring, I missed the land terribly, and with the support of Rose (a trouper and then some) we took over my father's farm.

I had the idea that I could be a gentleman farmer-writer. A modern Wendell Berry. I would be a literary man during the cold, quiet months of winter but lead the healthy outdoor life in the summer, cultivating corn and pitching alfalfa bales. And of course in autumn I could hunt with impunity. But there were several flaws in this plan. First, I had forgotten how much work farming really was—especially the dairy cows, which give no weekends off. As well, this was the early 1980s, when interest rates were at record highs—a nearly impossible time to start farming. In addition, Rose and I inherited Carl, my parents' hired man; he had been with our family most of my life and much of his (he had no real family of his own) but was aging now, and his situation required, as Arthur Miller wrote in *Death of a Salesman,* that "attention must be paid."

Another complication was of our own making. Mary Jane had burned out on the high-fashion international life. She was earthy at heart and physically strong—had the same kind of raw beauty and strength as Willa Cather's Ántonia—and since I was desperate for help on the farm, we invited Mary Jane and her boyfriend to come live with us. She and Christian moved in to the sturdy, remodeled wooden granary (the same one wherein cousin Gerry and I had shot sparrows). We made a loose, share-the-wealth arrangement, and babies began to come quickly from both sisters. The rural route mail carrier brought leaky tins of olive oil from Italy, a subscription to the *Daily Worker* (both oil and subscription in care of Christian), as well as rejection slips for my short stories—but not for all of them. I slowly began to publish and win a grant here, an arts board award there. Once a handwritten postcard came in the mail. "I read your stories 'Flax' and 'A Gravestone Made of Wheat' and want you to know how much I enjoyed and admired them both. You're a fine writer and I wish you every bit of luck to keep on doing it." It was signed by Garrison Keillor.

Though the center did not hold on our farm experiment, for two years at least I was able to do it all—including get back to the woods with a gun over my shoulder. But Thomas Wolfe was right: "You can't go home again." At least not all the way.

Chapter Eleven

During my time away at college, and then in California and St. Paul, much had changed in my small town. Park Rapids had gotten its second stoplight—and then a third. In my youth there had been only one stoplight in all of Hubbard County. A McDonald's arrived, and soon after that Subway and Pizza Hut. There was talk of a Walmart. Smaller grocery stores and butcher shops disappeared in favor of big, wide-aisled, well-lit supermarkets.

The same great changes were happening on the land. Irrigation and potato growers arrived—along with a giant French fry plant where the descendants of homesteaders now worked in a roaring assembly line fragrant with and covered by a sheen of cooking oil. Central pivot irrigators, their long arms turning like the hands of giant clocks, sprinkled most of 160 acres in one circle—and tolled the end of the small dairy farm. The use of manure was replaced by commercial fertilizers (nitrogen and potash). Dry-land farming and natural weed control through crop rotation and fallow fields

disappeared under the wide-winged sprayers that misted At-
razine and Roundup.

Uncle Jim modernized. He took out a loan for two new,
blue, vacuum-sealed silos and a shiny, low, long dairy barn—
all of which required more intensive farming and more equipment. His great leap forward also had an unsettling effect upon
the larger family. My father and his brothers had always shared
farm equipment and labor—and argued about the same—but
now their disagreements became more complicated.

Uncle Emery, the oldest brother, was against everything
modern. He was slow-moving, slow-talking, slow to get his
teeth fixed—but not slow-thinking when it came to dollars
and cents and who owed what to whom. Uncle Emery was
"tighter than a gnat's ass stretched over a rain barrel," as
my father described him. Emery's singular skill was returning a tractor with a bone-dry gas tank or a plow that after
a couple of turns about the field suddenly needed all new
lays. During my two years of active farming, Uncle Emery
took me and my Stanford degree to the cleaners on every
exchange; he was so good at being cheap—raised it to such
an art form—that in the end I did not fully mind getting
shortchanged.

If Uncle Emery was dead set against modern farming
practices, my father was dubious. "Bankers are not your
friends," he always told me; he was pretty sure that no good
could come of Uncle Jim's big loans. He (my father) further
believed that Uncle Jim had fallen under the smooth-talking
spell of their brother Curtis, who had sold him the fancy
new silos.

Curtis was the youngest of the brothers and the one
who had traveled farthest from home. A Lyndon Johnson–

like figure, he was tall, with a strong nose, silvery hair, a Stetson hat, and his own Cessna. His voice carried a hint of honey from his years in Illinois, where he farmed, sold silos, and at various times had implement dealerships and his fingers in Chicago commodities-exchange trading. He was greatly admired by the great-nephews and younger cousins for his style—a built-in sense of confidence not unlike a retired general or an old college quarterback. Back in the day, Uncle Curt had once stolen a girl from my father "just because he could," my mother told me more than once (with some irony, this matter was a pebble in her shoe more so than in my father's). He also liked, she grumbled, to "Lord it over" his brothers. She thought of him as the golden boy, the only brother to go off to college while my father had stayed home to milk the cows.

Along in the 1980s, Uncle Curt's charmed life took a hit. On the wrong side of some commodities trades and with a couple of bad decisions by a son-in-law in a tanking farm economy, he lost most of his fortune. He had enough money remaining to buy a lake estate and two hundred and some acres of land contiguous to my grandfather's original farm—and so Uncle Curt, too, came home. Soon Curt's place became the family's center of gravity, a matter that further skewed the complicated arrangement of four brothers living in close proximity.

My father had less and less mobility for hunting. Uncle Emery had knee problems (or so he said) and couldn't walk much, plus he had vague problems with an ulcer. Uncle Jim had put off getting glasses and blamed his "damn rifle" for missed shots at deer. None of the four brothers' necks turned like they used to. None of them could physically hunt sunup to sundown nine days straight, and they were not happy about that fact—and whatever personal issues they had, they made sure to take them out on one another.

Our whole hunting dynamic had changed. Since I had "been gone for so many years" (it was not *that* long), there were unspoken questions about my commitment to the family. My cousin Gerry had had his fill of beating the brush for the older men and now mainly hunted with his own sons. In short, the extended family that once hunted with the efficiency of a pack of gray wolves—the Weaver Gang, as we were known locally—had collapsed. No more tight convoy of pickups speeding bumper to bumper around section roads. No more line of red coats fanning out across a cornfield or surrounding an eighty-acre woods. My cousins and uncles began to hunt out of their houses on their own land. Fence lines and boundaries became matters of contention. The tally of deer was no longer share-and-share-alike. It was each family for itself.

The return of Uncle Curt also brought a slightly weird competitiveness among the uncles for the allegiance of us "boys." It was not that they wanted us (Gerry and I, as of old) to beat the brush for them but rather they wanted to assert their power over each other. One issue particularly rankled my father. Curt gave the younger guys nudge-and-a-wink permission to shoot a deer "for the camp"—meaning an untagged, unregistered deer to eat during the term of the season. In my father's mind, this was a metaphor for Uncle Curt's life in the business world, and, while unsaid, he believed it was just deserts that Uncle Curt had taken his great fall. Uncle Curt blamed his losses on crooked bankers, but my father thought otherwise. Gerry and I wanted no part of these brotherly squabbles, but there was good news on the hunting front: by the 1980s, no one needed a large family of hunters to bag a deer.

For a few years in the early 1960s, deer were as scarce as four-leaf clovers. A pointed hoofprint in the snow was a big deal. Those seasons we drove the dirt roads looking for tracks, and if we found them, one of us—often me—jumped out and "got on it." We sent posters around and ahead to points where the deer might emerge or at least show its brown hide; others spread out on both sides of the tracker and pushed into the woods. Some seasons we hunted all nine days, dawn to dusk, exhausted and with groin pulls from wading in deep snow and chapped lips and raw noses from bitter cold—and ended up with only a couple of small deer. One November, discouraged by the lack of deer signs in farm country, we headed in our convoy of pickups to near Duluth, where we hunted in the timber of state forestland. The trip was not successful: we froze in our tents and got one small deer over three days. Statistics showed only one to two deer per square mile (640 acres) in some areas, which left, as my father said, "a lot of room around them."

In the 1980s, however, with changes in logging and farming and climate—especially from several mild winters—the deer herd rebounded with a vengeance. Motorists began to die in car crashes from hitting a deer or, more likely, from trying to avoid one; statistics showed more than twenty deer per square mile in some areas. This is when the hard work—and the art—of hunting devolved into shooting.

With a surplus of deer around, hunters got lazy. My uncles and neighbors no longer had to beat the brush or follow tracks, so they constructed elevated box stands at the corners of fields. Each enclosed platform, essentially a tiny cabin on stilts, had a propane heater, a slide-open window, and an easy chair—a mini-suite wherein a hunter could doze and listen to the Vikings on portable radio, then rouse himself in time to shoot a deer that materialized at the edge of the woods. My father was dead set against this kind of hunting. He hated box stands in general—thought they were a lazy man's way to hunt and an eyesore besides. But he reserved his full disdain for tree stands. "Only monkeys hunt in trees," he told me.

When I was sixteen or so, and on a rare occasion when I was posted before a woods rather than fighting through it, I climbed high into a Norway pine in order to see over the brush before me. The higher I climbed the colder it got, plus the northwest breeze made the tree sway ever so slightly— not good for taking a steady aim. Waiting for the drivers to appear, I began to shiver and then freeze for real; when I finally gave up and clambered down (making sure, with my stiffened limbs, not to fall and shoot myself), two deer burst out exactly where they were supposed to. I was halfway down the tree, with my rifle slung over my shoulder, and I didn't get a shot. I lied about not seeing the deer but learned my lesson.

By the 1990s, bagging a deer or two no longer required much skill or time. This worked well for me, a busy father-writer-teacher, but there were losses. All the skills my father had taught me—patience, especially—were no longer necessary. Deer hunting became opportunistic and brief; often I let several smaller deer pass my ground blind rather than disturb the universe of the woods. And then there was the matter of buying special permits for extra deer— an unheard-of total of five in some years. Who needed five deer—essentially a whole pickup load of venison?

On the other hand, a high deer population made it easier for older hunters such as my father and uncles to stay in the game. By 1990, my father was confined mainly to his pickup (around his yard it was an electric cart, and inside the house, a wheelchair); this required him to get a special hunting permit for "the disabled." I, more than he, was irked at the labeling, but he was philosophical and each year sent in the proof required for his license. He was discreet about hunting from his truck and shooting out of the window (his brothers joked about him having it "easy"); he never parked where he could be seen from the county road. His declining physicality also required adjustments to other areas of his hunting life, including his gun.

Young hunters start out with lighter-weight rifles; old hunters end their careers with the same. My father, in later years, was good about hiding or at least not fussing over his fading physical powers; while often abrupt about what he needed, he was not a whiner. But after going from wheelchair to electric cart he lost a lot of arm strength and upper-body mass. For most of my hunting life he had shot a .30–06 Remington Model 742, a medium-weight rifle of serious caliber; it was a carbine, short with heavy recoil—had a real kick. We shot identical guns, and I learned early on to tuck its stock tightly into my armpit and lean forward when shooting to let my legs and torso roll with the blow—or else I woke up the following morning with an aching, black-and-blue shoulder. (At an outdoor shooting range I once saw a man lean his sighting eye too closely into the telescopic sight on his own .30–06; the recoil rocked him backward and gave him a gashed, bloody eyebrow.) In my father's arms the .30–06 looked larger every year.

He could not stand up to shoot by then, so during deer

seasons his gun barrel poked out the window of his black Chevy pickup. My mother and I fashioned for him a small sandbag that we draped over the truck's windowsill. The soft, conforming sand helped him steady his aim and kept him from having to lift the full weight of his rifle.

By 1992, it was usually just the two of us hunting. My son, Owen, age nine, was not old enough to hunt, but was "getting there," as my father put it. So, with two rifles but only one set of legs, my father and I developed new strategies. Depending on wind direction, he parked his truck in tall weeds at the end of a field or backed into the brush at a logger's landing in the woods. I circled far around, then still-hunted—tried to push a deer out to him. It was my favorite kind of hunting: move as slowly as the long minute hand on a clock; stop minutes at a time to watch the woods ahead; move again a hundred feet; pause to listen. If I could hear my pulse beating in my ears, I was moving too quickly. The goal was to get a deer to move—but not bolt. Jump up, maybe, and bound off a few yards but then walk, all the while looking over its shoulder.

In the densest oak and aspen patches I sometimes crawled, keeping an eye ahead for a buck's antlers woven into the branches' deadfall or for the flicker of a white and brown ear from a deer still curled in its bed. The key to any kind of hunting was to see the prey before it saw you. If not, the chance for a good shot was usually gone. Nothing was more pleasing than jumping a deer—seeing it bound up from its bed, its white flag waving off, then slow to a trot as it headed toward my father's gun.

On one occasion, when my father was eighty, I still-hunted the big pines toward the old logger's landing where he was parked when a small buck sling-shot itself from fallen oak leaves and ran forward. I straightened up and counted: *one thousand one, one thousand two, one thousand three*—then came the *chak*-POOM! of his rifle. I hurried forward.

In the clearing I saw his black pickup but no sign of my father inside. I rushed up and looked into the cab. He was sprawled sideways on the seat, rifle askew on the floor.

"Dad! You all right?"

He sat up groggily.

"What happened?" I said. Then I saw the sandbag: it had a burned crease across it; a tiny, pale stream of sand flowed from it like a broken hourglass.

"I don't know," he mumbled, rubbing his shoulder. The recoil of the .30–06 had rung his bell; I had a momentary, cartoonlike image of the cab full of chirping tweety birds.

"Did you hit him?" I asked, meaning the deer.

"I don't know. Maybe," he said as he recovered his wits. He pointed through the window toward the woods. "He came out over there. I took a crack at him . . ." His voice trailed off.

When I was sure my father was all right, I headed to the thicket where he had pointed. The buck, a small four-pointer, lay just behind, dead on the oak leaves. I dragged the deer back near the truck so my father could see him.

"Nice one!" I called.

"I'm not sure what happened," my father said. He had noticed the scorched and broken sandbag; he looked chagrined, embarrassed.

"Don't worry about it," I said. "You got him."

He watched me position the deer and take out my knife. "Do you need any help?" he asked from his window. He made no motion to get out of the truck.

"No," I said. "I'll take care of everything."

For one of the first times in his life, he only nodded in agreement.

I took my time dressing the deer, making sure to lean aside so my father could watch. Could see everything. Could comment if he felt the need, but he didn't speak. It was the last deer he killed with that rifle.

For the following season he went to town and on his own bought a brand-new, lighter-caliber .243 Remington semi-automatic with a telescopic sight. "My eyes aren't what they used to be, either," he explained, the "either" a clear reference to the incident of the sandbag, the open window, and the .30–06.

"Plus it will be the perfect rifle for Owen," he added. "It'll be his when I'm all done hunting." In indelible marker, my father had written my son's name on the gun case.

Chapter Twelve

I killed my first deer when I was thirteen, which was not remarkable by age—many young hunters nowadays begin as young as eleven or twelve, and Daniel Boone, after all, "killed him a bar when he was only three"—but in anyone's hunting life, the first deer killed blooms unceasingly in the garden of memory. I taught for many years in the English department of Bemidji State University, and there my freshmen students often wrote "First Deer" essays. Their writing on the topic was predictable and not very good. And because part of my aim as a college teacher was to move students off their small-town or rural dime, I set rules.

"You are allowed only one hunting essay," I informed them early on in the semester (someone always groaned at this bad news), "so make it a good one." And then we talked about the assignment—primarily narrative and descriptive writing—and about how to "make it real." As a primer, we often read Tim O'Brien's story "The Things They Carried" or something similarly well written and afterward took a close look at the imagery. On one occasion, when the students just were not getting the concept of sensory detail, I brought to class a box of florescent markers, and we color-coded O'Brien's prose: pink for visual imagery, green for what can be heard, blue for smell, purple for touch, and so on. When we finished, O'Brien's pages looked like a garden of wild-flowers. "Oh! I get it, Mr. Weaver," my students said more or less in unison. However, the best image of student deer-hunting life came not from an essay but from an overhead conversation in the student union. A young woman student settled into a table of girlfriends, one of whom asked, "Didja get your deer?"

"Yeah," the arriving student answered and gave a brief summary of "my doe." Then she looked at her hands. "But I always treat myself to a manicure when the season is over," she said. "Deer blood is so hard on the cuticles."

In my family, the idea of my sisters hunting never came up. Deer hunting was understood to be a father-son kind of thing. Nowadays in Minnesota, girl deer hunters are no more remarkable in the woods than girls on the basketball court or soccer field. Fathers are spending time with their daughters, teaching them how to shoot and hunt and paddle a canoe and cast a line. From my former perch in public education, I have found that girls who hunt and enjoy the outdoors are generally more self-actualized than girls who do not: they are more confident, more decisive, and far less self-conscious about their appearance. I would also bet the farm that outdoor girls are less likely to have internalized psychological issues such as anorexia and cutting, not to say lesser addictions to shopping malls and pop culture. For young women who have killed a deer, boy bands and movie magazines don't measure up.

Still, in my day, age thirteen was a watershed moment for boys, our Quinceañera, our debut into the society of men.

Thirteen was the year when I could have a real deer license and carry a real rifle.

My weapon in 1963 was my father's fine old .30–30 Model 94 Winchester. It was a short-barreled, multipurpose rifle of the kind that cowboys kept in saddle scabbards. The gun held seven cartridges, had a lever action that ejected the brass empties out the top, and had a tricky "buckhorn" open sight—the only aspect of that rifle I did not love. My father had moved up that year to his new Remington .30–06, but I could not have been happier carrying his old Winchester. It felt good in my hands—had a walnut forearm as thin as a boy's wrist, a comforting loop for my trigger hand and finger, plus a balance not easily explained—not so much weight as a harmony of motion, of heft in the hand. I was never prouder than to walk away, out of sight of my father, "my" rifle at the ready, toward my own deer stand at the edge of my own field.

Actually, it was a neighbor's field, Mr. Wenger, who did not hunt so much as we Weavers but did not post his land against trespassing, either. My father and I had hunted together near home all that day, with no shots fired. Now we planned a "sit" until sundown.

The view from my stump commanded, south, a field of about ten acres and the woods that bordered it. To my right (west) was a narrow channel of woods, about thirty meters wide, with another small hayfield just beyond.

I tried to sit still—to move only my eyeballs—as the light fell and dusk gathered in the woods like fog. At one point I was certain I saw a deer at the edge of the treeline. But, no. I had conjured it from oak leaves (the ears), saplings (legs), and a single knothole for an eye. I lowered the Winchester and let out a breath—which is when I looked to my right. Through the trees was an actual deer, not big, standing head down and feeding in the other field. Heartbeat roaring in my ears, I raised the Winchester. Gun barrel waving of its own accord no matter how tightly I held it, I drew back the hammer to full cock, took as fine a bead as I could with the curved, buckhorn sight—then fired.

The rifle jumped—as did the deer. It bounced straight into the air, came back down, looked around in puzzlement, then returned to feeding. I blinked, then took a breath, levered in a fresh shell, took closer aim, and fired again. Same result. The deer bounced again straight up as if on springs—but landed startled and uninjured. After a brief spell, it lowered its head again to the alfalfa.

I shot once more with the same result—after which I realized that I had to get closer. I got down on my belly and crawled—and none too quietly; the deer looked in my general direction a couple of times but always returned to feeding. Finally, from about fifty feet away and from a prone (and steadier) position, I fired again. The deer buckled and fell in a heap. I rushed forward to find a "button buck" brown-sided on the green grass, a yearling, breathing its last; soon my father appeared, limping quickly through the trees.

"I got him!" I shouted.

He put a finger to his lips—being quiet was one of the biggest lessons of hunting—but he was smiling.

As he dressed out the little buck, I explained how I had had trouble with the buckhorn sight and so sneaked up on the deer for a better shot.

"Sneaked up on him!" My father was so amused as to be almost speechless. He couldn't stop smiling. "I think you two were made for each other," he said, as he wiped blood from his hands with a handful of oak leaves.

Chapter Thirteen

After my failed experiment as a gentleman farmer, it was time to get serious about career and family, which now included two children, Caitlin and Owen. I had things to teach them about the outdoor life, but first I needed a job. A part-time teaching post came open in the English department of Bemidji State University, which was only fifty miles up the road. I took it. My starting salary was $15,000 per year. I commuted for the year or a bit more that it took to wind down the farm operation, and then Rose and I moved our little family to Bemidji.

I was not unhappy with the small, friendly city of Bemidji, the first on the Mississippi River. It was a college town with eagles overhead, unfenced yards in the neighborhoods, and cheerful day-care providers. One of my secret worries on the farm had been for the safety of my children. My mother has stories of near calamity, including the time I disappeared as a toddler, turning up in the back cow lot of the dairy barn; the thousand-pound Holsteins were just coming home from the pasture for milking, and each one gracefully stepped over me where I sat on the barn-door sill. I don't remember that. And one late March day when the fields carried small lakes of snow melt, my sisters launched me, Huck Finn style, on an old barn-door raft onto one of those cold, vernal ponds; the water was peat-dark from manure runoff and looked really deep. My parents arrived home just in time to rescue me, though I remain convinced that I was in good hands with my sisters. There were also tractor tires to run over children, and power takeoffs and grain augers and open hay mow doors and silo gas—no end to the ways one can be injured or die on the farm. It was a relief, honestly, to see my little family settle into our small, rented rambler in a starter-home neighborhood of southeast Bemidji.

I concentrated on teaching, writing, and being a good dad. For a spell of about a year and a half, the balance was perfect: I had one foot on the land (the farm was rented, but I could still visit and hunt there); the other was firmly planted in literature and writing. Our little house had an unfinished basement and a woodstove, and at my card table and electric typewriter I tapped away early and late the winter of 1984 on a family issue that would not fit into the teacup of the short story form.

After coming down from North Dakota to Minnesota, my grandfather Oscar bought a farm in eastern Becker County from a man who had bought the land from a timber company. No problem there; my grandfather bought the land fair and square. However, the 320 acres was originally part of the White Earth Indian Reservation, and in the 1980s, with the rise of the American Indian Movement (AIM) and the cultural rebirth across Indian land, the legal provenance of farms like my grandfather's was called into question. Many ended up in court. The Ojibwe tribal members, aided by lawyers from

AIM, asked a fairly simple question: why was 92 percent of the White Earth reservation land owned by whites?

Investigation of long-ago land transactions produced a serious legal matter for current owners: clouded title. This pall on land ownership spread fear and loathing among many of the white residents, especially the farmers; in their eyes, the mess was "all the Indians' fault." In the eyes of bankers, clouded title made land worthless—what can't be sold has no value—and soon farmers could not take out operating loans against their farmland, and little real estate anywhere on the reservation could be bought or sold. Which was sort of the point, the tribal lawyers maintained.

Racial tensions ran high. There were minor acts of violence and a pervasive sense that things were building to a head—that something bad and violent was going to happen. My grandfather's farm was within the boundaries of the reservation, and it was a time of great uncertainty for the Swenson family.

Red Earth, White Earth was my fictional rendering of this culture clash, and when I was partway along, I sent several chapters to a literary agent. Within six weeks he had an offer from a New York publisher, and then another offer. A bidding war ensued. The novel sold for a six-figure sum—a kind of golden monkey wrench thrown into the smoothly turning wheels of my little family's life in Bemidji. Not that I was complaining. But I had to finish the novel, then navigate its publication and book tour, both of which kept me apart from my family and the land about which I had written. One night during the tour, after finally arriving in New York City at the Algonquin Hotel, I had in my briefcase the *San Francisco Chronicle, Washington Post,* and *New York Times,* all of which I had bought up that day in their cities of origin.

I tried to convince myself that this was fun—that I was living an author's dream. But it was a bitterly cold night in New York City, and in my hotel room the frost on the inside of the windowpane, along with the weight of my coat atop the blankets, felt like my little eave bedroom in the farmhouse when I was a boy. I slept fitfully all night, not entirely sure of where I was.

The television movie of *Red Earth, White Earth* took me to Los Angeles, where I helped keep the script moving forward during a screenwriters' strike, and then to Montreal for some of the filming. The movie, a dehydrated version of the novel, came and went, though not before annoying just about everyone on or near the reservation. Dennis Banks and Russell Means of AIM vowed publicly to "come after" me. Local farmers thought they had been portrayed as rednecks. And everybody thought I had gotten rich at their expense.

About the same time, my short stories had begun to attract attention, and on one occasion I found myself in Washington, DC, for the PEN short story awards. They were held in the bowels of the Library of Congress in a wide and southern-appointed sitting room, where I ended up on a couch between then–poet laureate Gwendolyn Brooks and Joyce Carol Oates. Ms. Brooks was a tiny woman in a brightly colored African-type dress and a tidy hat above radiant dark eyes; Joyce Carol Oates had a lemur-like gaze and a pleasant though relentless manner of asking questions (a great conversational tactic when stuck beside a stranger). While eating finger food and trying to converse with them both, I got a cracker crumb stuck in my throat and had a coughing fit so violent as to alarm Ms. Brooks—who asked if she might fetch me a glass of water. I managed to signal that I was not dying, and hung in there to accept my award for a short story, called "Dispersal," about a farm foreclosure auction and a neighboring farmer in attendance who has his eyes set on a farm implement but can't stop thinking of W. H. Auden's poem "Musée des Beaux Arts." The story was a suitable metaphor for my life: half my heart was in books, the other half was still on the farm.

The writing award also highlighted a major irony: the better I wrote about the land and the woods, the further removed I became from them. Hunting was now opportunistic and rushed. If I got out partridge hunting once or twice in October, I felt lucky. I had not sat in a duck blind in years. For the deer season opener, always the first Saturday in November, I arrived late Friday night at my parents' house, then headed to the woods in cold blackness the next morning. If I got my deer right away, I skinned it and went home soon afterward. Proust, whom I have read about, believed that one has to let go of the past in order to write well about it, but this was not what I had in mind. Literary success also put a big dent in my grand plans as a father.

One October day when I was home for a stretch, Owen, then about six, was puttering about the house. It was a sunny day, and the late afternoon had suddenly opened before me.

"Hey, Owen—would you like to go hunting with me? Take a walk in the woods and see what we can see?"

He paused. Checked the clock. "I kinda want to watch *Reading Rainbow.*"

"You can always watch *Reading Rainbow,*" his mother said. She was in tune with my worries about the Weaver family's male traditions, and while she did not see them in such black-and-white terms as I did, she knew it was a growing issue—not only with me but with my father. Owen's eventual life as a hunter often came up in his grandfather's remarks. There was a calendar, a clock in his mind: teach Owen the ways of the woods before he (my father) was no longer able to hunt. I was greatly annoyed with Owen's response to my offer to go hunting but didn't press the issue. I certainly did not want to force him to go with me.

"Okay, then, see you later!" I said cheerfully, as if I were Tom Sawyer and hunting was a picket fence to be painted.

"Okay, Dad," Owen said in kind, and turned to his television show.

In a great funk, I took my shotgun and headed to the woods by myself. I hadn't hunted for some time, and on my brief ramble not far from town I stumbled upon a wood-lined slough full of mallards. After executing a stealthy, on-my-belly creep that was pure back-to-the-future (my high school buddy Jeff would have been proud), I jumped to my feet. The ducks exploded into the air, and I dropped two plump greenheads.

When I arrived home, Owen was in the yard shooting baskets on his Fisher Price plastic stand, weighted with sand in the bottom and with a breakaway plastic rim. He was left-handed, that was clear, and athletic besides.

"Hey, Owen, look what I've got!" I said proudly. I held up the greenhead ducks for inspection; their feathers glowed iridescent in the sunlight.

He drew up his play-sized foam basketball and held it to his chest. He stared. With complete earnestness he asked, "Don't ducks have rights?"

Chapter Fourteen

In a dark corner of my heart I blamed my children's attitude toward hunting on *Sesame Street* and *Mr. Rogers' Neighborhood*. Those two programs, along with public television's kids' shows in general. All were urban-based, urban-produced, with an ethos that had nothing to do with rural life and certainly not with hunting. Guns, if ever mentioned, were scary and bad.

On the other hand, I knew by experience that television shows were about Nielsen numbers, and since hardly anybody lived on a farm anymore, it was not logical for Mr. Rogers to stop by the barn to feed the calves and afterward ramble off with his .22 to shoot gophers. Nor was Mr. Rogers going to show kids how to clean a fish or gut a deer or set a snare for a coyote or find wild berries that were good to eat. "If he had to work for himself, he'd starve to death," my father used to say about men like Mr. Rogers. Soft men. Men whose ambition was suspect. Men who had no discernible survival skills if the going got rough.

My father often used the phrase "the fat of the land." It meant anything that could be gleaned, picked, fished, or hunted—and put to good use for the family. In the spring we speared suckers in a creek and had them smoked (neither my mother nor Carl would eat them). In summer we picked wild blueberries, chokecherries, pincherries, plums, and cranberries; blueberry bogs in July, when the mosquitoes and wood ticks and deerflies were at their peak, made for the worst kind of stoop labor—but my mother transformed the dusky blue berries into wine-dark pies and sauces better than any other kind. Some years, when they were worth good money, we picked pinecones. I climbed high up into the crowns of big white pines, up where the breeze soughed, and eased out as far as I dared on the pitchy, thinning limbs; with a stick I whacked loose the rust-colored cones. They tumbled down intact, and we gathered and sold them by the bushel basket to the local, state-run tree nursery. My father gave us kids all the money we made picking cones—a lesson not lost on us. He also helped me build a frog box, a small, wood-framed rectangle with wire mesh on three sides and a strip of inner-tube rubber tacked across the top with a slit in it. He waited on a pond bank, smoking, while I waded and pounced, waded and pounced along the edge of a slough as I filled the box with small- to medium-sized leopard frogs. We took the frogs to town and sold them to bait shops, which in turn sold them to out-of-town bass fishermen too lazy to catch their own. We fished for bluegills, sunfish, crappies, bass, northern pike, and walleye on the water or through the ice. And of course we hunted partridge, duck, geese, and deer in the fall.

Whenever I came from the university back to the farm for a weekend or on spring break, my father always had jobs waiting for me. In the space of a few hours I went from a class on James Joyce or a poetry reading by John Berryman to the close, low-ceilinged dairy barn. From books to a fork and shovel. Sometimes my task was to clean a calf pen—pitch the sodden straw through a small window and into the manure spreader just outside, my eyes stinging from the ammoniac smell of calf piss—while other Saturdays I climbed the cold chute of the silo and threw down several days' worth of pungent, fermented silage. In March he had a firewood permit waiting, and for several days we cut down standing dead timber and sawed it up. But on the coldest weekends of winter, I helped my father with his trapline.

He had always trapped, so this work was nothing new to me, and there was a practical reason for the trapline: income from my father's fur trapping paid for much of my university studies. A half-dozen red fox for sixteen credits of literature. One prime, buck mink for *The Collected Poems of Dylan Thomas*. There is a photo of my father and me on snowshoes beside his black Chevy pickup with our catch of the day. I have carried the three frozen coyotes and one fox over my shoulder out of the woods (I look slightly warm and out of breath). The temperature is below zero. We are posed for my mother's Kodak, and the stiff carcasses are outstretched as if running or leaping—but caught, freeze-frame, in midair.

There are other trapping photos. These I took myself. One is of my father crouched in snow beside a dead black Angus. We have dumped the steer, which died by natural causes, perhaps a twisted gut, in the edge of the woods, and my father is setting traps around it. He is sprinkling—carefully!—brown cattail fuzz inside the open, black, iron jaws of a number-three jump trap. The cattail fiber, beneath a fine sifting of snow, will keep the trap mechanism (springs, pan, and trigger) from freezing open. His arm is outstretched as if making an offer to the dead animal, though it was making an offering to us.

There is another photograph, taken by me, of a red fox in a leg-hold trap. The fox is alive but tired. The background is white snow. Diagonally across the lower part of the frame is a fallen black sapling on which the trap's drag has hooked itself. The tight chain stretches back to the trap that is clamped upon a reddish-orange blossom of meat and fur, which is the fox's front left leg. The fox has been chewing on itself. Only a few thin cords and tendons remain before it would be free. Squatted in the snow, the fox strains against the chain and away from the camera. There is a dull look on its narrow, pointed face. The perspective of the photo is taken close to the ground, at fox height.

When I was a boy, it was exciting to clamber down the road bank to check a mink trap or, in deep winter, wade through waist-deep snow to a snare set just out of sight of the road—and come back to the truck dragging a rock-hard coyote. Trapping was full of strategy, stealth, and expectation. In William Faulkner's story "Barn Burning," the father, Abner Snopes, is a horse thief; he has been wounded in the Civil War and has a limp from a musket ball taken in the foot while thieving (he stole horses from both sides, Union and Confederate); and Faulkner describes Snopes as building "chary" fires with only a few small sticks of wood in order to escape detection by soldiers. Trapping with my father also had an undercurrent of "theft" about it—not because we ever did anything illegal but because of the way we went about it.

Most trappers hiked deep into the woods and along the streams, carrying a Duluth pack heavy with iron traps, axe, wire, and other gear. Their goal was to set their traps where no other trappers visited. My father could not walk far or carry much of anything (I was his full set of legs). As well, there was nothing to help him get around—in the 1960s, snow-mobiles were rudimentary and undependable and all-terrain vehicles had yet to be invented—so he was forced to set his traps a short walk (or crawl) from his pickup. Unable to compete with the other trappers who used "the shank's pony," as my father called walking, or risk getting his truck stuck in backcountry snow (there were no cell phones then, either), he set traps in broad daylight. Where a culvert gurgled beneath a well-traveled township road. In a trickle of a creek within sight of a country home. Where a fox trail crossed the main highway and disappeared into the woods. "Hardly anybody looks to the side when they drive down the road," he said. "Most people just don't see things."

On winter Saturdays when I was young, we drove the country roads and looked for tracks. For crossings. I became expert at identifying animal prints. A fox steps only where it has stepped before, a single line of paw prints unwinding across the snow like a necklace of gray pearls on an invisible string. Coyotes are less efficient, make a heavier trail—especially when the snow deepens. All animals follow natural topography, including curves and slopes of terrain that eventually draw them into natural channels and "pinch-points": a narrow ridge between sloughs, the base of a sharp hillside, water flowage of any kind. "Animals move like the wind," my father once said, "along the path of least resistance."

I nodded. I was very young and didn't quite understand the phrase, but I liked the sound of it; I said it again and again inside my head as we drove along.

Sometimes the more public the set, the less likely it was to be discovered. We trapped close upon the city limits:

beneath a busy bridge, at the base of a railroad trestle, along the river. Sometimes this entailed subterfuge that bordered on a guerrilla operation.

"I'll slow down and you hop out," my father said, but I knew the drill. With trap, hatchet, and piece of frozen duck in hand, I got ready. My father timed it until traffic had passed and then accelerated forward. I eased the truck's door ajar. As he braked at the bridge (or underpass or trestle), I bailed out and slid down the bank as he drove on. After making the set, I skulked along the ditch, then reappeared a hundred yards farther down, back on the shoulder.

"Lots of tracks down there," I said as I climbed back into the warm cab. I said this even if I saw none; it did not seem like a bad lie.

"I figured so!" he said, his eyes full of light. After a couple more such under-the-nose-of-the-public forays, we usually repaired back in town to the bakery for a fresh, cherry Bismarck and milk for me and the same with coffee for him. But then we had to go home and skin our catch.

While some animals such as fox and coyotes were sold to the fur buyer in the carcass, beavers and mink had to be skinned and fleshed. A mink's hind legs, with pelt peeled away, were as difficult to hang onto as greasy chicken bones— and were three times smaller. Mink also had a scent gland near the anus that, when nicked, stung my eyes and nose as if a skunk had sprayed.

When that happened, my father always said, "Hold on— we're almost done."

And I always did.

During college, when I was bigger and stronger, I sometimes pulled him on a sled. A cheap, plastic kid's sled worked fine and allowed us to range farther from the road, like "a real trapper," as he said once. We trapped along open fence lines with thin scatterings of trees among which fox and coyotes crossed. Here we used snares. When positioned, their dangling, pear-shaped, black loops hung open to the size of a powder-room makeup mirror—perhaps smaller than you would imagine. Strategic placement of branches or dried weeds (thistle stalks worked well) narrowed the trail: the goal was to make the fox or coyote lower its head to duck beneath something—and into the braided iron loop.

A snared animal thrashes the site in a tight circle, around and around, tearing away snow down to brown grass and then dirt. The bare ground is a bull's-eye in the snow—as if a small bomb has exploded. The animal chews on the wire. Breaks its teeth. Tears its mouth. The greater the animal's struggle—the harder its lunging—the tighter the wire.

With my father riding behind on the sled, often with a dead fox or coyote across his lap, I labored back to the pickup, my breath puffing silver in the January air, my eyes squinted or sometimes fully closed against the brilliance of sun off snow. The only sounds were my snowshoes—the *shush* of dry snow under gut mesh and the creak of ashwood curves. In my watery gaze the black truck was a portal, a door, an escape hatch in the all-white landscape. And in late winter, when the trapping season ended, it was time to meet the fur buyer.

"Old Plotnik," as he was called, was a small man with a big nose, wiry but ageless and with a tendency to sigh as if the world were arranged specifically against him. I do not recall ever hearing his first name. He was a fur buyer for someone "bigger than me," as he said, probably from Chicago, where the furs went to be tanned and then sewn by immigrant women (probably Russians) into fur coats for

Oak Park dowagers. Plotnik came to Park Rapids on a regular circuit. He rented a cheap room at the Rainbow Inn motel where he met his trappers—"my boys," he called us (yet another clever trick of his—to suggest that we were all in this together, that sacrifices must be shared).

"He probably lives in a mansion," my father muttered once, but it was clear that he liked the man and looked forward to the haggling with *Mr.* Plotnik, as my mother insisted I refer to him. If the weather was moderate, twenty degrees or above, trappers lingered outside the motel door, smoking, talking, waiting their turn, joking about "the skinning room" (a description my father also used for bankers' offices) and what tricks Plotnik had up his sleeve this year. As the trappers waited, Plotnik hefted carcasses and held pelts up to the light. He liked to see furs in the daylight, but in very cold weather we brought them into the motel room that was pungent with the tallow smell of raw furs, and tobacco, and the trappers themselves, whose wool coats smelled of animal musk, chainsaw oil, and wood smoke. Beaver "blankets" draped chairs. Muskrat skins rose up in a dun mound in the corner. Frozen fox and coyotes in the carcass were brought in for inspection, then taken back out to Plotnik's refrigerated truck.

Under a lamp he leaned close into our catch, especially my father's mink. "This one's rubbed," he sighed. "What a shame!"

"It's not rubbed that much," my father replied.

Or, "Looks like you nicked him," Plotnik said, squinting closely at a mink's hide and a tiny knifepoint hole—then clucking his tongue at the great loss to both my father and himself.

"But prices are good this year, I hear," my father said.

This brought a shudder from Old Plotnik. "Oh, no!" he said, glancing up. "They're down again—way, way down!"

My father always laughed when he heard those words—the same line we heard every year—and he could mimic them quite closely after we went home to report in to my mother. The trapping cash was his money; she did not expect him to tell her the amount, but the air in the house was always brighter and more cheerful after he had sold his winter catch.

Chapter Fifteen

Our new house (thanks to my first novel) in Bemidji was situated on a gravel street on the west side of town. The neighborhood was mixed, with a Republican city councilman on one side and a traditional Ojibwe family on the other. There were no fences, and lawns were made for kids' play, not grass. Caitlin and Owen walked three blocks to elementary school, and we did not worry about stranger-danger. It was small-town living in all the best ways. However, our social life tended toward college teachers and literary types—none of whom hunted or had much connection to the land—and slowly, inexorably, Caitlin and Owen became "town kids."

If Owen's future as a hunter was increasingly in doubt, my ability to influence my daughter's life was also largely gone by the time she was eleven or twelve. Caitlin was drawn more and more into the drama of middle-school life but maintained her own personality (she had some of her grandpa Harold in her). By age thirteen she made her own dental appointments and attended to family infrastructure items such as ordering call-waiting for our home telephone. It is not that her mother and I were bad parents; rather, Caitlin was a girl who liked to be in charge of her own life. Hunting, however, was Dad's and Grandpa Harold's thing. She didn't mind it; she just wasn't interested. Our outdoor dad-daughter time was hiking and bicycling and lots of basketball—serious front-yard hoops—usually followed by a trip to the Dairy Queen.

I still held out hope, however, that Owen would hunt. There is a rare photo of Owen with a gun. It's my old Daisy-brand BB shooter. He is aiming (left-handed) at a paper target while I stand behind him holding back my father's Chesapeake Bay retriever. When Owen got taller, I introduced him to my battered .22 rifle. The sharp, whipping report of the little long gun made him flinch at first—as a small boy he had always disliked loud noises—but he soon enough became a passable shot. One summer Saturday at his grandpa Harold's house, I brought out a shotgun. It was a twenty gauge, a nice, lighter-weight gun without a lot of recoil. I fitted Owen with earmuffs, and first we shot a paper target just to see the spray of pellets, then a green tomato just to see it explode, then a clay pigeon set up as a stationary target. Fun, guy stuff.

"Now you're ready to shoot one in the air," his grandpa called from his electric cart.

Owen looked dubious.

"Your dad will show you how it's done," Grandpa Harold said confidently.

I helped Owen load a clay pigeon into the hand-thrower and showed him how to launch it—a quick flick of the wrist.

"Pull!" I called.

He threw; I swung and fired. I missed the first one but exploded the next couple.

"Now you try," Grandpa Harold said to Owen.

Owen did but had no luck on the first one. Nor on several consecutive discs. He looked crestfallen and embarrassed and soon rubbed his shoulder.

"That's enough for today. You'll get one next time," I said.

"I doubt it," he muttered.

On two or three occasions he and I tried again, but Owen could not hit a clay pigeon. This was a boy who could sting the palm of my catcher's glove time after time from our backyard pitching mound and who had a silky-smooth, three-point shot on the basketball court.

"Not a big deal," I said. "It will happen someday."

One fall afternoon when he was in seventh grade, I got him to go partridge hunting with me. I would carry the gun. He had been noncommittal about taking a gun safety class and so did not have his official badge, as did most boys his age, a round patch sewn onto his hunting coat and worn with pride. It was a grand October day—the motley of maple and oak and birch leaves would be enough, I hoped, to hook him on the woods. We were walking down a quiet trail, slowly getting into the hunting state of mind (I thought), when two hunters, one large, one shorter, appeared walking toward us. A father and a son, who was about the same age as Owen. I got a sinking feeling.

We met on the trail. "Any luck?" I asked.

"A couple," the man said.

"I got 'em both!" the kid said quickly.

"Good for you," I replied.

Then the father looked at Owen. "Hey, you forget your gun?"

Owen glanced at the man; the other boy, holding his shotgun, stared at Owen with a greatly superior look.

"He doesn't have his gun," I said stupidly.

"No gun? What's the matter, don't you hunt?" the man pressed Owen—then laughed heartily at his own joke.

"Not everybody hunts," I replied. I wanted to say more but was full of rage—which along with a loaded gun in my hand was not a good combination. "Let's go, son," I said, and walked on.

Owen hurried to catch up with me.

"What a jerk," I said presently.

Owen had no reply; his shoulders slumped as we continued down the trail.

We soldiered on, eventually flushing a bird. As I swung to fire, from the corner of my eye I saw Owen jerk up his hands to cover his ears.

As November approached, the matter of Owen going deer hunting—or not—grew in drama. Owen was evasive; I was noncommittal with my father.

"Did Owen take his gun safety course?" my father asked.

"No. Not yet," I answered.

Silence. "Well, it's not like there's a game warden going to check us."

I didn't reply.

"I bought some slugs for the twenty gauge," my father said. "It should be a perfect starter gun for him."

"I'll tell him," I said.

Back home, I did.

"I probably have basketball practice in November," Owen replied.

But on the last Saturday of deer season I got him to come with me to his grandfather's house. He was getting big enough and tall enough—had some whisker fuzz by then—to be more clear about his likes and dislikes. And it was clear by his silence and his posture that he wasn't happy about going deer hunting. *Please—just do this for your grandpa,* I wanted to say but did not. Which, in retrospect, was a parenting victory. And it was a larger family victory for my father to see Owen and me heading off into the woods dressed in blaze orange.

My goal was to show Owen how to track a deer, and not far from his grandparents' house we spotted a buck's hoofprint heading north. Our land lay to the south, but the neighbors across the road didn't mind an occasional foray across the fence, so Owen and I crossed over—which was also a chance to show him gun safety with barbed wire. Sans rifle, I crossed over the wires while he (gingerly) held the gun; then he passed it to me and crossed the fence himself. *One of your great-great uncles was killed doing this.* But I didn't mention that; the goal was a fun, upbeat hunting experience.

The afternoon sky was the same pale white as the snow-covered ground on which we followed the deer tracks, which headed north, onto a neighbor's land where I seldom ventured. He did not mind me hunting there, so we followed the tracks as they traversed ridges, knolls, and ravines. My focus was as much on Owen as the deer tracks (they were easy to follow in the snow); the afternoon turned dusky, and the tracks eventually disappeared among too many other prints—which was the perfect time to call it a day. I had no intention of shooting a deer even if we saw one; introducing Owen to the woods was a delicate matter, and I wanted to move slowly. No abrupt and thundering rifle report. No blood trail in the snow. Thinking such thoughts, I looked around and realized we were lost.

Not seriously lost. More "turned around." Owen and I were in a square-mile woods with farm roads on all sides, which meant if we kept walking in a straight line we would come out somewhere. But I did not know the line—the direction home. I *would* have, had I been hunting alone and paying attention to the sky and the light and the breeze, but that was cold comfort now.

"Well, enough for today," I said easily. "The buck got away. We'd better head back to Grandpa's house."

Owen brightened at this news. "Which way?" he asked.

"Well," I said in my most casual and confident voice, "we could follow our tracks, but we've been meandering all around—so we'll just head straight home. This way."

After a half-hour tramp we came out to a highway—on the far north side of the section. Now we were two miles or more from home, and it was getting dark.

"Where are we?" Owen asked.

"I think we went in the wrong direction," I said, and manufactured a chuckle.

He was silent. "How will we get home now?" There was a faint note of concern in his voice.

"No problem," I said. "We'll stop at that house up ahead and call Grandpa Harold. He'll come get us." I kept my voice light and cheerful, as if we were having a grand adventure.

We set off along the road toward the nearest house (a half-mile ahead), but before we got there a vehicle came along—a pickup full of hunters. I discreetly flagged them down. They were amenable to giving us a lift, though we had to sit on the rear tailgate, which, with swirling snow, made for a cold ride home.

"Any luck?" my father asked as we thumped into the porch of the warm house that smelled of roast beef.

"We trailed one, but he got away," Owen said, quickly shedding his parka. He did not mention getting lost; it seemed to be no big deal to him.

"Well, that happens," my father said, greatly pleased. "You'll get a crack at him next time."

The following year Owen had his own garage band (he was the drummer), and he made it clear that he preferred to stay in Bemidji and hang with his friends while I hunted deer. So on Friday afternoon I packed up my Jeep and headed down to my parents' place. We had sold the family farm by then but retained sixty acres, mostly timberland, where Arlys and Harold had built a new, smaller house. I arrived in time for supper; my father was waiting at the door, an expectant smile on his face. I suppose he thought Owen was right behind me, blocked from view and carrying a duffel bag of hunting gear—but when he understood that I was alone, his face fell.

"Where's Owen?" he asked.

I paused. Looked straight at my father. "He didn't want to come with me."

"Didn't want to come?" my father repeated. It was like I was speaking Russian.

"I don't think Owen is going to be a hunter," I said.

Chapter Sixteen

The Swenson side of the family made one contribution to the Weaver side that my father greatly admired: a recipe for mincemeat. He did not question how the non-hunting Swensons might have come by venison, which was a key ingredient, but made the preparation of the minced fruit and meat concoction a major family ritual. "Nothing better than a mincemeat pie," he said. So every other year, not long after deer season, we gathered for a Saturday to make mincemeat. No one was excused, and while Caitlin and Owen muttered about missing a Saturday with their friends, they came along and pitched in.

The recipe called for a peck or more of apples (peeled); several pounds of lean, cooked, and shredded or ground venison; five pounds or more of raisins and currants; a gallon of sweet cider and several cups of meat broth; two bags of brown sugar; a couple of pounds of suet; and spices including salt, cloves, cinnamon, allspice, and zest of lemon to taste. The goal was up to fifty pint canning jars of real mincemeat (not to be confused with "mince," which was fruit only) for use in pies, bread, and even muffins. The suet component in the recipe gave away the historical role of mincemeat in our family: a high-fat, high-energy winter food perfect for farmers, hunters, and loggers. During his winter work cutting spruce bolts, my grandfather Oscar probably ate his lunch by a snapping bonfire over which he warmed a large slab of mincemeat pie—then took up his Swede saw again. Except that now in the twenty-first century, we were no longer a family of farmers or loggers. Against the protestations of my father, over the years we gradually reduced the suet and tinkered with the fruit ratios and the spices. The recipe has notes and reminders from decades past as, like California winemakers, we always tried for that vintage year.

On mincemeat-making days, Owen ground raisins and currants through an old, shiny, Wardway hand grinder. Caitlin turned apples on a newfangled miracle peeler that issued a single, long filament of peel per apple. I weighed ingredients and chopped and spelled Owen on the grinder while my father, in his wheelchair, kept track of the proportions as they went into a giant, cast-iron cooking pot. It was messy, fragrant work; Caitlin and Owen fooled around with necklaces of apple peels, or fashioned them into drooping mustaches, or flicked raisins at one another.

The fruit preparation (my mother had precooked the meat) took most of the morning, after which the kids were excused and the adults pressed on with the cooking and canning. The bulk and volume of the raw mixture in its cooking pot required a laundry stick or a freshly peeled aspen limb to stir. Which was my job. As with maple syrup production, the cooking could not be rushed. The goal, with continual stirring, was gradual heat toward a low, slapping boil—like a miniature, bubbling geothermal pot of Yellowstone Park. During the stirring the kitchen filled with the scent of cooked fruit and cinnamon, and there was a time to talk and hear stories about the old days; though Caitlin and Owen had finished their parts, they usually hung close by to listen and laugh or sometimes ask their grandparents questions about how it was back then.

By day's end, after we had cleaned the kitchen and the bright jars sat all in a row slowly cooling from their hot-water bath, their lids, like crazy little clocks chiming, went *ping!* and *ping-ping!* as they sealed. We kept count—and the kids cheered when the last one rang. Making mincemeat with my children was not hunting, but it was the next best thing.

When it became clear that Owen did not like guns, I took another tack in his outdoor education. Canoe trips to the Boundary Waters Canoe Area Wilderness were a good introduction to the bush, and a fly-in trip for walleye in Ontario gave him a taste of fishing camp life. But a couple of hiking trips in Montana were key. A friend and I put together a series of dads-and-lads trips to the Bob Marshall Wilderness in Montana, Glacier National Park, and Banff National Park in Alberta. Hiking and tenting in bear country was perfect for the teenage boys: enough danger to give them something to talk about back home; backpacks heavy enough to make for serious hiking; mapping and tenting for good lessons in outdoor living; and mountain passes and vistas the bigger reward—that and coming back down the mountain with hot kneecaps and rubbery legs to make it, just barely, to the trailhead and the Jeep.

It was also on one of these trips that Owen learned a lesson about preparation. He was fifteen by then and through some complication of our schedules had to catch a ride with another dad and lad, who were to meet the rest of us in Waterton, Alberta. I guessed that Owen would wait until the last moment to throw his backpack together—and that he most certainly would forget things.

The late-arriving contingent landed in Waterton on schedule, and we drove to Banff and the trailhead and prepared to set out. Except that Owen had forgotten his hiking boots. We all looked at his sandals. I said nothing.

"I guess I'll have to hike in these," he said sheepishly.

"Looks that way," I said.

There is a photo of Owen, with full backpack, moving across a snowfield in socks and summer sandals. But at lunch break, as he massaged his wet feet, I removed from my backpack a spare set of boots.

"Would these fit?"

The rest of the fellows laughed like crazy.

"You had these all along?" Owen asked, looking at my old Red Wing boots.

I nodded.

"So—this is some kind of lesson thing?" he asked sarcastically. He was over six feet tall by now and was not smiling.

"Yes," I said.

"Okay, got it," he said—and took the boots.

Hardly a half-mile down the trail, he and his buddies were laughing about the incident. I heard Owen murmur something about ". . . Grandpa Harold, too."

And the boys giggled again.

It was these kinds of outdoor adventures, along with Owen's athletic life in school, that buffered for me—and my father—the fact that Owen would never be a hunter. In time, his grandpa liked nothing more than to be parked in his wheelchair along the baseball fence to watch Owen pitch or lay down a bunt or to attend a basketball game. He was just as happy to sit through a middle-school band concert where Owen's drumsticks flew as fast as a partridge's wings.

There were, in the end, no regrets. None about "Owen's deer rifle" that he would never shoot. None that he would never be a woodsman.

"But we'll keep the gun," my father said to me. "Someone will use it someday."

My father died in July of 1998, when Owen was fifteen. That he reached age eighty-five was something of a miracle; in addition to his post-polio issues he had heart problems as well as colon cancer. He wore "the bag" for the last several years of his life, a burden graciously attended to by my mother. I was with him in the hospital at the last—it was my shift—and I always felt glad, even blessed, for that experience. I am also glad that my sisters and mother did not have to be there to see it.

Over the twilight hours and then into the warm summer night his breathing labored, his breaths rattled. I kept one hand on his forehead and the other on his needle-bruised forearm. His eyes were closed. I kept talking to him. Speaking to him softly. I said again and again, "We're getting there, you're doing it, we're not far now." Had someone been passing in the hallway, my words would have been mistaken for birth coaching, as comfort for a mother in labor. At the moment when his congested lungs finally over-labored his heart, he sat half upright—a jerk of his upper torso—then fell back with a long sigh. He lay still. Within seconds his complexion shaded to a waxy yellow.

I sat for many minutes—possibly ten—listening to the murmur of the night nurses as they passed outside the door. I was blank with grief, but I did not want to lose this moment. They were minutes out of time. Finally I went to tell the nurse.

"He's gone," was all I could muster.

Somewhere in William Faulkner's writing is the phrase "a successful funeral." My father's was not. Or at least not fully so, what with his religious conversion perhaps not completely felt by him or by the two male preachers who presided. They seemed mostly interested in preaching to the assembled—did not even give a full account of my father's life such as one would find in an obituary—and during the service I grew increasingly angry. I felt my father's sharp-edged anger rise up against those cocksuckers, as he once called the preachers. But in deference to my mother I sat on my hands and made sure to hold my tongue afterward.

After the interment, we gathered back at my mother's house. Changed out of our funeral clothes. Drank coffee. Tried to relax. I was spent, but Connie, always the organized one, soon began talking about "getting things done while we kids are all together." There was clear logic to her point—both of my sisters lived out of state, Judy in Nevada and Connie in California—but neither Judy nor I stirred or replied.

"I know it's soon, but what things could we do today?" Connie persisted. "We might as well do it now, because if we don't, you'll have to hire someone after we all leave," she said, turning to my mother.

My mother's gaze slowly traveled among her children and young grandchildren, then rose upward, to the wall behind the couch.

"There is one thing," she said. "The taxidermy."

Lining the wood paneling were two deer heads, white-tail bucks, along with an array of pelts from my father's years of trapping: one fine specimen each of otter, beaver, fox, and coyote. Beautiful, shiny furs along with two trophy bucks.

"What about them?" Connie asked.

"They should go," my mother said, dully but resolutely. "They'll only remind me . . ." Though of what she did not say.

We all looked at each other; I was the only one in the family who hunted anymore.

"Bud," my mother said, turning to me and using my family nickname.

"Sure," I said, with a glance at Rose, who nodded ever so slightly. "We'll take them."

"Well, let's get them loaded up," Connie said, beginning to bustle about.

"I'll do it," I said sharply. For reasons not fully clear to me I didn't want anyone—even my sisters—touching the pelts and mounts, most of which I had helped field-dress or skin and the rest whose provenance I knew, including the buck from The Cut. We pushed the couch aside and then I carried the pelts and mounts one by one to my car, which was already somewhat full of changes of clothes and leftover funeral food—plus I needed to save room for Caitlin and Owen. I laid the furs carefully below the rear window; the deer heads I arranged as best I could in the back seat. Later, with the antlers and glass eyes and polished brown noses looking out both side windows, and with Caitlin and Owen squeezed uncomplaining among the deer heads, we drove to Bemidji. We were a car crammed full of the living and the undead.

With my father's passing there was a hole in the woods. An empty space. In a perfect world his place would have been filled by Owen. Some extended families are so rigid about the tenure of deer stands—the hereditary rights to The Ridge or The Oak Narrows or The Old Car Body—that hunting rights pass like the throne in a monarchy: when the king dies, everybody moves up one chair. But this was not our family because now I mostly hunted alone. I was the last hunter.

There is something to be said for going solo into the woods. Complete freedom of movement. No one to think about or worry about. A full, undistracted immersion into nature. But in the end, hunting alone is no fun. I began to mull over inviting Gerry's boys to hunt with me, but too much water had passed under the bridge for that. Gerry himself had arthritis and bad knees from his years as a retail milk-truck driver, from lifting the thousands of crates, from the continual climbing in and out of his refrigerated truck. My old friend Jeff was a longtime member of a big hunting camp and could not walk so well either these days. But a hunting partner—who was also family—came from an unexpected direction.

Connie's son, Michael, had spent part of several summers at "Grandpa's new house" when he was a kid. My father taught him about tools, about lawn mowers, and some about guns. But Michael grew up in California and had never hunted anything. After a hitch in the air force and a deployment in Turkey, he came back to California with a new appreciation for family, for roots—and announced his intention to come back to Minnesota and go deer hunting. This was a shock to us all. Michael even bought his own deer rifle, "just like Grandpa's," but there was no real reason to risk its transport in airplane baggage; after all, Owen's rifle was available.

Michael's first couple of seasons intersected with the end of my father's hunting life, when he was wheelchair-bound, so it was largely up to me to help Michael learn the ways of the woods. Which took a while. A burly truck driver in his thirties by then, with a buzz cut and a belly, Michael had a heavy boot on the trail. He crunched and snapped every branch he passed. As well, he had the habit of chewing a sweet, pungent brand of snuff and spitting in the snow around his deer stand.

"Michael, if I can smell that stuff, a deer can, too," I told him.

While he did not stop chewing, he brought along a plastic bottle for more discreet expectoration. He also tended to overdress, then overheat when walking, then get chilled when he sat on the stand for a couple of hours—which was a long time for Michael. I understood the need to get up and move but was often surprised to see him come clattering through the woods behind or in front of me. Still, I was happy to have someone to hunt with, and I worked hard on Michael's behalf. I posted him in prime spots, then tried as of old with my father to push a buck Michael's way. On one occasion, the action on Michael's rifle was not fully closed. "I kept jerking on the trigger but nothing happened!" he said, greatly chagrined, and described the small but nicely antlered buck.

"But now you've learned something," I said, trying to make light of it.

"That's for sure," he replied with a trace of a smile.

On another occasion he was looking the wrong way and didn't see the deer. On yet another, he saw the buck, had a good shot, but just plain missed. Which bothered him more than me.

"That's all part of hunting, Michael!" I said as we searched for blood but found nothing.

Back at the house for supper, we recounted our day in the woods to my father, who lay on the couch with a blanket over him. He spent most of his time there now.

"I can't believe I missed him," Michael said to his grandpa.

"There's no end to the ways to miss a deer," my father said with a glint in his watery eyes.

My father died that summer, and I knew the first November season without him was going to be tough. As October came, and the leaves flamed and then fell, and the dun and grays of November appeared, I felt increasingly adrift. Sluggish. As if I were swimming in increasingly cold water. But Michael was coming back to Minnesota, and so I had to muster.

I dutifully went to my mother's place on Friday, and there had our usual hunter's dinner of roast beef and gravy. But my father's empty chair was too much; during my mother's grace I broke down. Michael was the tough guy. "Here, Uncle Bud," he said, handing me the steaming bowl of potatoes. "These will help."

When the alarm buzzed at five AM, I didn't want to get out of bed. I didn't want to bundle up and head off into the cold, purple dark and freeze my butt off sitting on a stump. I just wanted to sleep—and probably would have had Michael not been there.

I gathered myself to cook us a hunter's breakfast, bacon and eggs with toast and jelly and a pot of strong coffee for my thermos. Michael soon clumped up the stairs from the basement. He disappeared outside for a few moments, then stepped back in and said, "Wind's from the south."

Checking the wind direction was something I always did first thing but this morning had forgotten.

"But no stars," he added. "Looks overcast."

"Good," I said. I tried to generate some enthusiasm as Michael talked through where he might post up: the options for him should I come through here or there, this brush patch or that oak grove. It was understood now, with several seasons under our belt, that I was the deer mover and shaker, that Michael was better off, with the scoped .243, being on the stand—or, in our case, on his campstool behind a brush blind.

Before heading to the woods down different trails— Michael's went south, mine went east—I paused to whisper confirmation of the schedule: meet back at the house at nine-thirty to warm up, have a cup of hot cocoa, and figure out our next move.

I was back in the house by nine, chilled more than usual and with nothing much to say to my mother, who bustled around cheerfully and was finishing baking blueberry muffins. Eventually Michael's boots thumped in the garage; he had seen no deer either.

The woods the rest of the day were as empty as if all the wildlife had been sucked up by a giant vacuum and deposited in the next township. I did not see a deer, a partridge, or an owl. One lonely raven passed overhead, croaking once and turning his neck to look down at me as he flapped by. A couple of squirrels rustled, and a few chickadees pecked. But that was all. By day's end I was stiff and cold and exhausted. I ate too much roast beef and pie for supper and went to bed early.

The next morning I felt hung over. Drugged. It took all of my powers to get up, get dressed, fry bacon, then pull on my wool pants and parka. My rifle weighed twenty pounds. And again, nothing moved in the woods and our midmorning snack might as well have taken place in a funeral parlor.

When we headed out again at nine-thirty, the sun was bright, the snowy trees and oak leaves dead still. No wind, crunchy leaves—the worst kind of hunting conditions. On days like this, deer bedded down and stayed down.

Michael, it's no use. Let's head back to the house. That's what I wanted to say. And my mouth opened to speak those words, but something stopped my tongue. Tied it in a full knot. I felt paralyzed, at some kind of tipping point. The rifle in my hands was heavy with the weight of generations of Weaver men, men who threw a shotgun or a rifle over a shoulder and headed off to the woods, men who ranged easily for miles, as I had as a kid, a gun held naturally and lightly in the crook of my arm, back when the fields and woods were open before me—but maybe those days were over. Maybe this was the end of the line.

I looked at Michael. He waited for direction. Had he not been there, I would have turned and gone home. "Okay, here's what we're gonna do, Michael," I whispered.

We walked together to a fork in the trail. The paths diverged around a ridge dense with gnarled oak and blowdown. We agreed to stay on the trails; with a "quiet" woods, if we set a boot into the front of a brush patch the deer would bolt out the rear. There was a faint, easterly breeze.

I pointed Michael down the trail to the east. He nodded and made a waving motion, meaning that his scent would drift through the blowdown. We had gotten better with hand signals, with intuition of one another's movements. As hunting partners, we had made much progress.

He carefully walked on, his boot steps lighter these days, better at treading heel-to-toe, heel-to-toe.

I moved ahead a few yards to position myself on the west side of the ridge. I waited.

Michael was barely out of my hearing when branches crashed as if a dead tree had slammed down. There was a tremendous racket—and then horse-heavy running sounds. I threw up my rifle, pressed my "off-safe" button. The crashing sounds slowed as they neared a clearing.

A massive buck, head up, rocking-chair antlers erect, stopped at the trail—deer always look both ways before crossing any open space—the biggest deer I had ever seen. An easy shot, too, as if he were offering himself up. But suddenly the big buck floated and danced in my sights—became a standing-moving target. After over forty years in the woods, I had buck fever.

I could not draw my front bead fine enough in the rear sight (the butt of the rifle stock was likely not far enough into my armpit), so I took a breath, held several inches low, and fired. Dust and hair puffed high up on the buck's back; his spine broke like a suspension bridge collapsing, and he went down in a thrashing, bellowing heap. I dropped to one knee for steadier aim, and as his big neck flailed side to side I squeezed off another, killing shot. Then the woods were quiet. "Michael!" I yelled.

The buck was one of the best taken in the county that year. A wide, tall rack of antlers, fourteen points in all, and 227 pounds. When Michael and I took it to town to be registered and weighed, we drew a crowd on Main Street. The deer also made the local newspaper. There is a photo of me in the back of a pickup holding up the buck's head; I have made sure his tongue is in his mouth and there is no blood on his white muzzle or neck. The title of the article is something like "Fictional Buck Comes True," and the brief text refers to my father as "having a hand in it." I don't remember saying those words, but the reporter knew me, my father, and my whole family, as did most everyone in our small town.

Chapter Seventeen

I had always wanted to take my grandpa Weaver's Model 12 Winchester back to South Dakota—shoot just one pheasant with the old gun—but there was never time. After my father passed, the need to complete that circle became stronger and stronger. Though my literary, married, and parenting life had tightened its velvety noose ever more on my schedule, I recently arranged to meet my old friend Jack for a late-season pheasant hunt in South Dakota.

Jack had lived for many years in Alaska, where he taught English in the villages and hunted big game with the Inuits. Each Christmas he sent me a jar of home-canned, smoky-tasting salmon along with dead animal photos, as my wife calls them (Jack with a moose or a mountain goat or an elk); I sent to Alaska a Minnesota deer hunting photo or two, along with a jar of mincemeat. We had not hunted together for far too long.

On a bright, early December day, I drove southwest from Bemidji through snowy forest and lake country, passing just north of the Ponsford Prairie where my mother had grown up. The table-flat farmland with its thin, sandy-loam soil was spotted with central-pivot irrigators, one per quarter-section of land. They are what make the crop circles—most of 160 acres—that one sees from an airplane window at thirty thousand feet. At ground level, each irrigator had a long pipe, supported by stilt wheels, that stretched drooping but stiffly across a field. Giant, iron centipedes that drink millions of gallons of water over the course of a summer. Irrigators were just coming into use when my grandfather reached the end of his farming days (he never milked more than twenty cows), and he did not think much of them—certainly never imagined having one on his land. My uncle Claron and his son Jon farmed together for a while, but the dairy cows soon went, and the land passed eventually to Jon, who leased it to a potato farmer who immediately drilled a well and installed a "sprinkler."

I thought of driving past my grandfather's place but could not make the truck turn that way. I had not gone back since a day twenty-some years ago when I came to take him to the old-folks home. Somebody had to do it—it was time, we all agreed—and I volunteered so that my parents would not have to. Grandpa Swenson was not sure where we were going that day but did not mind so long as I, his own "Buddy-boy," was driving. It was winter as well, something that turned out to be a gift; when we arrived at the rest home in the small town of Menahga, the wake of a passing snowplow had mostly covered the sign that read "Green Pine Acres Nursing Home."

I pressed on in my black Chevrolet truck through rolling country around Detroit Lakes and then to Fergus Falls, just west of which the land flattens to fields of soybeans and corn. My goal was I-29 south, the borderline freeway between

Minnesota and the Dakotas. After several hours of cornfields, I arrived in tiny Faulkton, in central South Dakota—and our rendezvous at a hunters' motel. The hodgepodge of the Westside Motel, 1950s vintage, had a single-level main unit, some cabins around back, plus a "hunter's house" next door. Jack's hunting party had rented the house, plus a couple of cabins besides; it was a long-time, annual trip for them.

Used to hunting mostly by myself or with Michael, I was wary about the party—and the partying—aspect. But, as Rose said when helping me pack, "You need to do this trip."

The pheasant hunters rolled in at cocktail time, Jack and his older brother Mike, along with a gang from Minnesota. We sorted out sleeping arrangements at the motel, which had a game-cleaning station out back—a long, knife-chewed countertop with portholes over garbage cans that were half full of pheasant heads, entrails, and tail feathers. We repaired to the Legion for a beverage, then to the only steakhouse in town for dinner. The rest of our hunters ranged from dentists to mechanics, with various subsets of grammar, outdoor gear, and capacity for alcohol. I sipped a light beer. Hunting and alcohol never went together in my family.

Jack and I stayed up late getting caught up on our lives— both of our fathers were gone now—but pheasant hunting in South Dakota begins at ten AM, a civilized hour for hunters as well as birds.

In the morning I brought out my own shotgun, the brush-battered Remington 870 pump. Since these were gun guys and we had a little time to kill, I showed them some rust spots on the Remington. Asked their advice.

In unison, they shook their heads sadly.

"Once you get a spot, it never goes away," one fellow said.

"The only thing you can do is keep it oiled," another added. He brought out a small can of Hoppe's gun oil, the sharp smell of which took me back to my grandpa Weaver's house in the run-up to hunting season. A kitchen table loaded with guns, cleaned and oiled—taken care of—and ready for the hunt.

After breakfast at a local café, we left town in a convoy of four trucks in which we raced up a section-line road, surrounded a dry slough, then sent in the dogs. I hung back. Pheasants thrummed upward—"Hens!" someone called—but the roosters, with longer tails and dark-auburn coloring, were fair game. Shotguns *thump-thumped* and roosters fell—or not. Dogs, Golden retrievers and black labs, worked the grass and cattails and emerged with limp, fiery roosters.

Some of the best hunting habitat is abandoned farmsteads, which South Dakota has plenty of. There is hardly anyone home in South Dakota. One place had a big, old farmhouse, empty, with a faded American flag and some peace symbols still hung in an upstairs window; a broken-backed barn and leaning outbuildings; a metal machine shed still in use by someone (inside, a field sprayer applicator with wide, extendable wings folded in alongside the chemical tank); broken concrete foundations where some other shed used to stand—and the entire farmyard overgrown by knapweed, common tansy, and Canadian bull thistle. We approached the waist-high jungle of prickly dry weeds like deer hunters with brush: post shooters on the far side, then send drivers and their dogs into the thick of it. On this push the drivers waded through weeds, shotguns held high and horizontally as if the men were fording a river heavy with current.

I was posted on an opposite fence line, Jack on my right, with sharp, pale corn stubble and patches of glinting ice stretching away behind us. The birds began to flush. A brilliant rooster came straight at me—not a good angle—and anyway I had to wait until he passed so as not to shoot toward the drivers. I tracked the chortling rooster, led him and fired. He folded and bounced onto the frozen field. I missed the next and the next; the remaining birds that flew past were hens. When the drivers were all out, I went to retrieve the bird—held its hot, downy, rainbowed heft in my palm. At least my personal shotgun still worked.

After our late dinner of pheasant jambalaya, I brought my old Winchester into the main house to keep it warm. Jack said, "That's just like my old man's gun!" He held it, worked its action. Other hunters chimed in about their fathers, their family guns.

"Looks stiff," one of the hunters remarked of the Winchester's action.

"It is," I said.

He oiled the slides of the gun, which loosened its action a good deal. I gave the fellows the short version of the gun's history, my plan to use it tomorrow.

"You'd better be quick with that old thing," a younger guy said. It was a joke with an edge on it, the kind of pecking-order humor that men in a group feel compelled to use.

In the morning the old Winchester felt clumsy in my hands. Its barrel was longer than my Remington, and its safe button was positioned exactly opposite from the safe switch on my Remington. But the sun and the light and the cornfields were the same.

We strung out to push a long cornfield—to follow a row for a quarter-mile out to the posters—which required us to line up like deer hunters. Then, on Jack's hand signal, we pressed forward into the tall corn. Its sharp and brittle fronds were at face height; tangled, fallen stalks crunched underfoot. This late in the year, most of the fields should have been harvested, but wet weather had delayed the combines; hunting was always more difficult with lots of standing corn. At least 10 percent of this cornfield was blowdown, a loss to the farmer, which also made for tough walking—but was good for the pheasants. The snowy, narrow spaces between the rows were hieroglyphs of three-clawed pheasant tracks—so many birds, in wind-flattened stretches, that the pheasants had formed tunnel-like trails beneath the fallen cornstalks.

A hen flushed at my feet—whirred away out of sight. I walked on. Jack was somewhere to my right. His gun pounded twice, and two roosters soared past unharmed—and too quickly for me to shoot. It would not have been a good shot anyway; the problem with hunting in a corn maze was to drop a bird without losing it.

Another tricky part of being on "the drive" was to find the right walking pace: not so slow as to lag behind, but not so fast as to get out ahead of the other guns (when in doubt, choose slow). By the muffled gun reports in the field, I had struck about the right speed. Nearing the last third of the field, pheasant tracks thickened. I got ready.

A rooster burst up close ahead like a Fourth of July rocket—and another on my left. I dropped the first one and winged the second; it fluttered down, head up. A runner. A cripple. For the moment I concentrated on finding the first, dead bird. Since the corn around me was uniform and unending, I took off my cap and hung it on a stalk, a trick I had learned from my father while partridge hunting in brush; from that center point I walked back and forth in a widening arc—always keeping my orange cap in my periphery—until

I found my pheasant. It lay neatly outstretched between the two corn rows. A brilliantly painted bird, rust-colored and rainbowed on the snow. After retrieving my cap I looked briefly for the wounded pheasant but then had to keep moving. I dropped one more rooster not far ahead. The old gun worked just fine, and in exactly the right circumstances of flushing birds, a "triple" was not impossible.

As we neared the end of the field, guns pounded— fine shot *tchak-tchaked* among the cornstalks—and I stayed low and slow until I heard men laughing on the gravel road. When I emerged, most of the hunters were holding birds.

"You did it," Jack said, his eye on the pheasant tails hanging out of my jacket's game pouch.

I briefly held up the Winchester.

The younger guy who had commented on the old gun the night before gave me a nod and smiled.

I was scheduled to head home on the third day, and that morning, Dave, one of the organizers, counted out my quota of frozen, skinned birds. Like the old days, it was share and share alike. Dave said, "You held your own and then some. Come back next year, all right?"

"We'll see," I said. "But thanks."

Chapter Eighteen

Some years after my father's death and the removal of his animal trophies, I also took his traps—a heavy, wooden box full of them. Iron of all shapes, coiled springs, and sizes. There were large, square Conibears for beaver and otter; "jump traps" with serrated jaws for fox and coyotes; coiled snares; curved and sharp "drags" with their chains and their tethers of telegraph wire. The last of it. "It's best that you take the traps, or they'll just walk off," my mother said. She lived alone now, and though she had lots of visitors, some borrowed things and forgot to return them.

For a couple of years the box of traps gathered cobwebs in a corner of my garage. I kept them out of loyalty to my father and the ever-so-remote chance that if things got really bad (as in Cormac McCarthy, end-of-the-world times), I might have to use them. But mainly the traps took up space in the garage and in my head. One summer day I took the lot of them to a fellow who does metal sculpture. He and his young family lived a couple of miles down the road, where they ran a small greenhouse and general store; he was formerly an art teacher, and he and his handsome, earthy wife had a couple of lively, barefoot kids who sold vegetables from their garden and minnows from the Mississippi River—they were a family who could survive the apocalypse and be cheerful afterward. I was happy to give the dad some work. I explained my goal: to "retire" my father's traps but to honor him at the same time.

He nodded, his eyes brightening even as I spoke.

"You're the artist," I said. "Make something out of them."

"They should be welded open," he murmured as he looked at the jumble of iron. "They're not traps unless they're set."

A few days later I drove past and saw him sitting on a chair with the traps spread around him on the ground. He bent to reposition one of them, then leaned back to look again.

In the end he came up with two pieces, one a freestanding contraption that incorporated the remains of an old metal sled (I had told him of my father and I sledding on the winter trapline), which my wife assigned to the backyard. "The birds will love it!" she said.

I was chagrined—saw it as more of a conversation piece in the corner of the living room—but she was right. The other piece was smaller and very fine: five traps, their pans open and triggers welded, their chains looped and circled back to the curved iron drag. Rose liked this one. It now hangs in our foyer alongside my father's snowshoes; and I have an idea that eventually my daughter will like it too, and claim it.

Caitlin lives in New York City. Among my Minnesota family and friends, anyone traveling that way, or west to

California, and now south to Austin, Texas, where Owen lives, is fair game for the question, "Say, you wouldn't have room in your luggage for _____?" Fill in the blank with frozen venison, or wild rice, or high-bush cranberry jelly, or a jar of homemade mincemeat.

On a recent occasion, friends Linda and Kris had tickets to fly from Minnesota to New York City. The two lively blonds, one divorced and one widowed, were part of a large Lutheran church choir set to sing at Carnegie Hall (one can rent it, which I found slightly disappointing). Caitlin's apartment was on Eighteenth Street and Park Avenue. A thoroughly Manhattan girl with an MBA and a large job in microfinance that took her to places such as India and Brussels and the United Nations, she also kept her fast-typing, social networking fingers on the pulse of Minnesota life. She knew that the November deer hunting season had just ended, and she liked her venison.

"It's only about four pounds," I said to Linda and Kris. "Select cuts of father-harvested venison frozen in vacuum-sealed packages."

"No problem," Linda said. "Get it to us right before we leave."

On their departure day, I wrapped the hard-frozen packages in several layers of newspaper, which is better insulation than bubble wrap (never use foil, which sets off airport X-ray machines), taped them tightly, and delivered them to Linda's house.

"We'll text Caitlin when we arrive at our hotel," Kris said.

"And don't worry about a thing!" Linda said, patting my arm.

"Yeah, Mr. Worrywart," Kris added.

Their plane departed on time from Bemidji, and then Minneapolis, and arrived safely at LaGuardia. I kept track of it via an online flight-watcher site, my venison a tiny, blinking satellite creeping east across America. I was just beginning to relax about the family protein transfer when Caitlin texted. "Have to work late. Will get there as soon as I can."

"Please do," I texted back. I reset my mental meat-thawing clock.

As it turned out, Caitlin had to work very late at her office at NYU, and the Minnesota women had a rehearsal or a dinner or some such—and their hotel room, unlike motels in the Midwest, had no refrigerator. Certainly no freezer.

Linda and Kris, ever resourceful, went to the hotel bar, where they had a drink and chatted up the bartender. Explained the problem.

"Venison from Minnesota!" he said with interest (he was originally from Maine).

"Yes. And we're afraid it's going to thaw," Linda said. She is a handsome woman who dates a friend of mine, a lucky guy.

"I could talk to the restaurant manager," the bartender ventured. "Maybe we could keep the meat in the freezer for you."

"Perfect!" Kris said.

"And if this Caitlin doesn't come?" the bartender asked.

Kris and Linda looked at each other.

"Then I guess the venison is yours," Kris said.

The bartender shrugged. "This is New York City," he said. "Things like that happen all the time. People don't show."

Though not my Caitlin. She did not make it until the

next day, but I imagined her striding up Sixth Avenue in her bright scarf and tailored leather jacket and power heels as only a twenty-nine-year-old, single, totally wired and net-worked Manhattan girl can do; and afterward, bag of venison in hand, stepping into the street to throw up a stiff-arm to snag a taxi as if she had cast an invisible hook and line into the streaming traffic and yanked a yellow cab to the curb. Then home to her small apartment that, later in the weekend, would fill elbow to elbow, wine glass to wine glass, with lively, hip young people, most from somewhere far away (Indonesia, Connecticut, Russia, California), the entire place fragrant with venison and curry, or venison and fresh rose-mary, and loud with conversation. Food and friends, all with stories to tell. Among the professional young in New York, life is much about narrative.

Owen, a musician, is a graduate student at the University of Texas—a percussionist "professionally trained to rock," as he describes himself. He's a long-time vegetarian but will eat wild game and fish that I have killed and brought his way. This might be as much about knowing the provenance of his food as it is a gesture to me, but it pleases me at a deep level. He is a tall and lean and totally "green" guy, easy to like and with few earthly possessions to weigh him down—perfectly positioned to thrive in this young century.

And maybe food from home, be it venison or mince-meat or jelly or wild rice, gives my far-flung family a way to hang on to the past. Maybe its taste or aroma is the objective correlative—the "formula," as T. S. Eliot wrote, for our midwestern roots. But I'd like to think it's more than that: a ritual that binds and knits us together no matter on what coast or in what decade we have landed.

Recently my sister, Judy, a long-time English teacher, was heading home to Reno after a summer visit to Minnesota. At the local airport in Bemidji a security screener held up a jar of jelly he had found in her carryon.

"Oh, no!" Judy said in dismay. "My mother must have slipped that into my luggage."

The inspector gave the jelly jar a closer look, then unscrewed the lid for a sniff.

"Chokecherry," he said.

My sister smiled hopefully.

"Well," he said, after a quick glance around at the other inspectors, "we mustn't disappoint Mom." He slipped it back into her bag and waved her through.

I visit my mother, ninety now, about once a week or so. She lives alone in her country home just a mile from our old farm and is a hub of cards, letters, and e-mail traffic for our family that is spread across the United States. She also has more friends and visitors than she can handle. Her grandchildren come and go regularly, including Michael, from Reno, and my beloved nieces, Lisa and Shari, from California. Those two girls have three sons between them—West Coast boys to whom guns and hunting are as remote as the Milky Way.

A couple of years ago, Lisa and her son Andrew (about ten, then) scheduled a visit back to Minnesota during deer season. "I just forgot!" Lisa said at the time.

"No problem," I told her, but teased her about forgetting her Minnesota roots. "Michael and I will just do our hunting thing as usual."

Except that young Andrew was greatly interested in hunting—wanted to go to the woods with Michael and me "to see what you do."

I was fine with that.

"No way," Lisa said to Andrew. "Your dad would flip." Her husband, a computer-tech, Bay Area, fully enmeshed dad, wanted no part of Lisa's "Minnesota life," a matter that had always annoyed me. As a little girl on summer vacations to Minnesota, Lisa could thread worms on a hook and catch and gut bluegills as well as any farm kid.

Later that day Michael shot a small buck. This was a very big deal, especially to my mother, who wanted to get photographs. So, *en famille*, we bundled up and took my truck and trailer into the woods to retrieve the deer. Lisa was dubious— not about a dead deer but about Andrew going along—yet she could hardly say no; the boy had been confined to the house all that wintry day because of deer hunting.

Down in the brush, Michael and I managed to keep our audience back from the gut pile on the snow and the blood trail that led to it; we dragged the deer quickly forward and swung the carcass into the trailer. I kicked oak leaves over a few drops of blood on the ground. My mother took photos of us all looking down into the trailer; Andrew's eyes were very wide.

As were the deer's blank eyes.

Andrew picked up a small twig and touched the buck's brown hair.

"You better not!" Lisa said.

He ignored his mother. "Uncle Bud," Andrew said to me, "can I poke its eye?"

"No," I said sharply. "You have to respect the deer."

"But, Uncle Bud, you and Michael just killed it!"

The matter of Andrew seeing a dead deer caused Lisa big trouble when she got back home to California. Her husband went ballistic (Connie, between marriages, was living with them at the time and told me this). He thought that his son had in some manner been "ruined" and railed at Lisa, who remained calm and measured (one of her strong suits). She managed to assure him that Andrew was largely undamaged by the dead deer experience, while we back in Minnesota could only scratch our heads.

On a recent summer trip with his mom back to Minnesota, Lisa's younger son, Jason, noticed my old BB gun, which I kept handy to sting red squirrels at my bird feeder. He had shot it on a previous trip—an event which also got Lisa in trouble.

"Can I shoot it again, Uncle Bud?" Jason asked. He had flaming, carrot hair, like his mom; he was a great kid and a good baseball player, too.

"No," his mother said quickly.

"Could I at least hold it?"

Lisa looked at me and rolled her eyes; I knew what she meant. "It's not a good idea," she said to Jason with a pained look.

"Just once? Uncle Bud?" Jason begged.

I shrugged. "It's up to your mother."

"Okay, just once," Lisa said. "But only for a second."

He aimed it toward the river, then at a chickadee at the feeder. *"Pow! Pow-pow!"* he said.

Later I took Jason fishing. He spent some of the time in the boat texting his friends back in California, which meant his spoon kept hooking weeds, but I didn't mind stripping them away and helping him get his line back in the water. At least we were outside with a fishing pole in our hands and with loons calling and waves lapping and the sun shining. As we practiced casting, I wanted to tell him that when he was eighteen he could come back to Minnesota on his own and I would teach him how to shoot. That he could even have his own gun someday—that I had plenty of them. That when we got back to the house, I would open up my gun safe and let him hold all the old guns—one of which might be his someday. And I would tell him the story of the deer with one glass eye. And how his great-grandpa once got shot in the knee. And how his great-great-great-uncle got killed by a shotgun—that guns were not toys—but if he learned to handle them safely, he could go hunting with me. But I did not say any of that. Lisa didn't need any more trouble at home, and for now, at least, I did not want to be the crazy old great-uncle who lived in the woods by a river.

On the way back from the South Dakota hunting trip with my grandfather's old shotgun, I stopped at my mother's house. I wanted to present her with a pheasant and was happy to see no car or truck parked by her door. Sometimes it is difficult to have quiet time with her, what with so many people dropping by. She takes in mending in return for chores around the house and grounds, including snow plowing and roof shoveling in winter, and once when I dropped by, a rough-looking fellow whom I vaguely recognized was sitting at the kitchen table. My mother was at her sewing machine. He was drinking coffee but seemed slightly discomfited—sat pressed far forward on his chair—which is when I noticed that he was sitting in his skivvies.

"I took one look at the knees in these," my mother explained, glancing up at me from her humming sewing machine, "and I told him, 'You give me those pants right now!'"

The fellow shrugged and gave me a sheepish "what-can-you-do?" look.

On another Sunday visit to her house, this time with Rose, my mother handed me a faded, brown paper bag taped shut and addressed to my father. I knew immediately what it was.

"Where did you get this?" I asked.

"I was cleaning. I knew I had it somewhere," my mother said, pleased with herself.

"What is it?" Rose asked, leaning in.

"Your husband's hair," my mother said. "From 1972."

I carefully opened the bag and fished out a handful of dark brown curls with the faintest sheen of auburn in them.

"I don't remember your hair being that dark," my mother said.

"Well, it was," I said.

My wife patted the top of my head. "Was," she repeated.

"Son, you could have all this hair made into a wig!" my mother said.

"Or a really bad toupee," Rose said. She and my mother laughed together.

"And if anybody made fun of it," Rose added, "you could say, 'What are you talking about? This is my own hair!'"

"Very funny," I said to them.

But today the house was quiet, and my mother came to the door to greet me. I handed her a dressed and frozen pheasant.

"Thanks, son! I haven't eaten pheasant for years," she said.

"Don't save it—eat it right away," I said.

"It'll be enough for three dinners!" she said, hefting the bird.

"All the better," I said.

She wanted to know all about the South Dakota trip and about Jack, whom she remembered—even his red-and-black-checked shirt that was in "such bad shape" when he visited the farm in 1979 and which she mended. And also would I look at her computer? One of the problems with her regular flow of visitors, many of them odds and sods who conveniently arrived at lunch or dinnertime, is that they used her computer and somehow managed to screw up its settings.

After I got her machine squared away, she quickly sat down to look at her e-mail. A note from Caitlin in New York. From Owen in Austin. Connie in California. Judy in Nevada. Photos from my nieces. Brief thank-you notes from her great-grandkids. Cheerful greetings from former sons-in-law (five of them, between Judy and Connie, though both sisters are now settled and happy). An uplifting letter from a Worker who had just returned from India where he and his partner had been spreading the gospel; the preachers come regularly to stay with my mother, and help her, and I thank them for it. More mail from former neighbors. Internet humor sent by well-meaning friends. "I put that stuff right in the trash," my mother said.

There was also a pile of old photo albums laid out on the kitchen table, and after lunch we looked through them. She enjoys this greatly and has made many small, tidy notations in order to keep the facts straight. The faces and the dates. "I'm not going to be around forever," she said.

The albums were labeled by year. The oldest of them flaked dark chips of cardboard fiber when we turned their pages. With serrated edges, some of the black-and-white snapshots had light yellow blotches where glue had seeped through; the patches looked like sunlight behind gray-toned skies.

Photos of the old Swensons on the homestead farm; they lean away from the camera and each other.

A photo of my uncle Curt on the local airport tarmac beside his Cessna. My grandparents, Oscar and Ella, are with him, along with Uncle Emery, who stands straightly and proudly—as if the airplane belongs to him. Crowding into the picture is someone my mother does not know, which irks her. Uncle Curt wears aviator sunglasses and is looking slightly off to the side and upward to check the sky; this is the day he gave my grandparents their first ride in an airplane.

A photo of Caitlin, age eight or so, in big glasses, seated at a typewriter. She is typing and has turned to the camera, annoyed to be interrupted, her head full of faraway thoughts.

Lots of dead animal and fish photos. One has me in the rear of my father's pickup. This one is in color, and I am wearing my deer-hunting clothes. Owen, only a few months old, is perched in a baby seat atop a deer; the deer's heart lies off to the side. I am smiling widely. Another photo: Owen is four or so and holds up, very gingerly, a deer's severed head, a small buck.

"What was I thinking?" I murmured to my mother. "No wonder he wasn't a hunter."

She laughed and turned the page. "Owen was never a hunter," she said, "just like my father."

Before leaving I filled her bird feeders and checked the salt level in her water softener (added, along with a dishwasher, after my father died), then posed for a photo beside my truck. It is customary with my mother: one photo before leaving.

"It's too bad the pheasants are all cleaned," she said.

As a compromise, I posed holding the old Winchester.

"I'll send this on right away to your sisters," she announced as the camera clicked.

"I know that you will," I answered, and gave her a hug. The photographs would be in New York, California, Nevada, and Texas before I got home.

I braked at the end of her driveway and paused to toot the horn and wave good-bye—my custom. In the big side mirror of my truck she stood by her house, clutching her sweater together against the cold day, her pale white wings of hair the same color as the snow that curled from the eaves.

I still had an hour's drive back to Bemidji, but for some reason I was in no hurry. I backtracked a mile down the frozen township road that ran past my old stomping grounds. Just south of my mother's house was the railroad bed, now a paved recreation trail used by snowmobilers in winter and bicyclists in summer. At the crossing where Gerry and I used to meet there was a recent biking fatality, and one more at the next crossing east—"high speed crashes with cars," as the sheriff's report in the newspaper described them. I can understand why. I have seen the summer cyclists in their aerodynamic outfits powering themselves down the narrow, green channel of the trail, tires hissing on the asphalt, their eyes straight ahead, looking neither right nor left to the fields and forest, their earbuds in, filled with the hubris of the modern and the fit.

My family, too, has had its tragedies and death. Rose's two sisters died young, Josephine to breast cancer and Mary Jane the model to suicide years after she and Christian returned to Europe. Their parents, Vincent and Rosalie, are gone, too. On the Swenson side, my grandparents have passed, as has Aunt Helen and Uncle "Al" (Eldred). He and his brother Claron (like my mother, still in good repair) argued bitterly over eighty acres of my grandfather's estate and could not reconcile even on Uncle Al's deathbed. Most of the old timers on the Weaver side have died: my uncles Emery, Curt, and Earl; Aunt Thelma (my father's only sister) and her husband, Uncle Earl. The funeral for Carl, our hired hand, filled a big church on a bright January day when it was twenty below zero; I gave the eulogy for him, the last hired man, perhaps literally, in Hubbard County.

Uncle Jim is hanging on at eighty-five, though he can't hunt much and lives alone in an overstuffed house and should not be driving anymore. Gerry lives just down the road from my mother, but we do not see much of him. His milk truck rumbles off at three AM, and when he gets home he dozes in his chair and watches football. Once a year or so he drops off a fresh fillet of walleye or a few crappies for my mother. His sons hunt, though not like they used to.

Two giant cell-phone towers dominate the cornfields and timber of Weaver Land, or what remains of it, about 250 acres. One tower stands just east of my mother's place; another looms on the crown of a hill that overlooks our original family farm. Atop the cell tower a strobe flashes endlessly, day and night. When I'm on my deer stand (I finally built an elevated box, though with no door, windows, or heater), I make sure to turn my chair so that I cannot see its blinking lights.

This past spring I visited my father's grave to plant a red geranium, the flower he liked best. His plot is among a cluster of Weavers including my grandfather Moffet and his

father, Ephraim, whose Civil War stone leans and is flow-
ered by dark lichens, its etched script blurred and softened
by time. On that early May day the cemetery grass was thin
but greening, especially around the dark headstones and their
collected heat. Faded plastic flowers bloomed across the
cemetery, but none of those artificial ones for my dad. As
I was on my knees troweling in the plant, I looked up; only
a few yards away, set against the sunny, warm side of another gravestone, was a ceramic fawn. Yard art. A perfectly
rendered spotted fawn, legs curled underneath itself, head
down.

And then it blinked.

A real fawn, only a couple of days old. Lying in place.
Told by its mother, in deer-speak, to "stay"—which it would
do forever unless discovered.

I turned my face away; wild animals do not like to be
looked at. The doe was nowhere to be seen among the headstones and the lilac bushes, but she was not far off, this clever
mom. In the cemetery there was plenty of new green grass,
few visitors, and no hunting.

The Last Hunter is set in the Iowan Old Style typeface family. Book design by Daniel Leary. Typesetting by Allan S Johnson, Phoenix Type, Inc., Appleton, Minnesota. Printed by Sheridan Books, Ann Arbor, Michigan.